Language Attitudes, Clentity
Construction Ar

C000133839

Studies on Language and Culture
in Central and Eastern Europe

Edited by
Christian Voß

Volume 44

Giustina Selvelli

Language Attitudes, Collective Memory and (Trans)National Identity Construction Among the Armenian Diaspora in Bulgaria

PETER LANG

Berlin - Bruxelles - Chennai - Lausanne - New York - Oxford

Bibliographic Information published by the Deutsche Nationalbibliothek
The Deutsche Nationalbibliothek lists this publication in the Deutsche Nationalbibliografie; detailed bibliographic data is available in the internet at http://dnb.d-nb.de.

CALOUSTE GULBENKIAN FOUNDATION

The author and publisher would like to thank the Calouste Gulbenkian Foundation for supporting this publication.

Cover Illustration:
© Giustina Selvelli

ISSN 1868-2936
ISBN (Print) 978-3-631-88446-1
E-ISBN (E-PDF) 978-3-631-88447-8
E-ISBN (EPUB) 978-3-631-88448-5
DOI 10.3726/b19946

info@peterlang.com - www.peterlang.com//

Dedication

This book is dedicated to the memory of Mrs. Malvina Manoukyan and Mr. Rupen Chavushyan, to my great grandmother Irma Seminati Gasparian, and to my beloved city of Plovdiv.

Preface

I will never see you,/ A near-sighted Armenian sky,/ And will not squint/ Looking at Ararat's tent,/ Nor will I ever open/ In the library of clay authors/ A hollow book of a wonderful land,/ From which the first people learned. (Osip Mandel'štam, Journey to Armenia)

The subject of this book has been growing inside me for a long time, has undergone changes and transformations, but can ultimately be traced back to my interest in Armenian culture, triggered by the sight and "impression" I had many years ago of its peculiar alphabet, which never ceases to amaze me with its beauty. The Armenian alphabet, like the other non-Latin-based writing systems I was learning, posed something of a challenge for me, not least because one day I did not recognize it on a sheet of paper on which it was written along with other languages of the Ottoman Empire. It was written in lowercase instead of uppercase and seemed quite different, unrecognizable to me, a perception I sometimes still have today. The "esthetic" question merged with the practical one in the question of how far an alphabet can be not only a representation but also a means and a function of a culture.

My approach to the subject was shaped by a strong personal interest in the topic even before I began field research. As a child, I discovered Armenian culture through a famous Armenian composer, Aram Khachaturian, whose pieces I played on the piano: this triggered my fascination and the emergence of a very imaginative childhood fantasy about Armenia; later, when my father told me that his grandmother was an Armenian from Constantinople, a city to which my Italian ancestors had moved in the mid-1800s, I discovered that I was also a bit Armenian and began to feel a personal calling to the subject. Then, when I learned about the Armenian Genocide—called Medz Yeghern in Armenian—(thanks to the music of the American-Armenian rock band, System of a Down), I was very shocked and wondered why we were not taught about it in school.

All this somewhat romantic talk about the history of my Armenian component serves to highlight the emotional, perhaps idealistic, component that binds me to the subject at hand. And thus the biggest problem I faced was not to exaggerate my subjectivity and try to use a kind of privileged bifocal view from "inside" and "outside" the community. I decided from the beginning to declare my "Armenianness" to the Armenian community in Plovdiv, and strangely enough, many of its members suspected it by claiming that my face was undeniably Armenian! No one could understand why I was so interested in them unless it was because I too was Armenian. The funny thing is that during my first encounters with local members of this community, my once-stated percentage of Armenianness ("one-sixteenth") gradually increased from mouth to mouth that after a few minutes one person asked me, "So you are half Armenian, your father is Armenian... do you speak Armenian at home?" And I had to explain that I was only minimally Armenian, and that Armenian was a language I studied at the university and wanted to try further in Plovdiv, but no one in my family spoke it (to find out who spoke it, you have to go back to my great grandmother and her ancestors). This did not cause any disappointment; on the contrary, almost always the last sentence was, "No matter what the percentage, you are Armenian and that's it!... As we say, one drop is enough to make you Armenian!" If I had to summarize in a few lines how the issue of my identity developed within the community, I would undoubtedly describe it as a progressive intense "Armenization": in a way, I almost assimilated more than I integrated, which is paradoxical given the premises regarding the dynamics opposing assimilation in the Armenian diaspora (Panossian 1998: 151).

My slow acquisition of the Armenian language through participation in Armenian classes for children and youth made me even more "familiar" in the eyes of the community members and its main representatives and also allowed me to experience firsthand what it means to learn a language with such a difficult alphabet. This allowed me to put myself in the shoes of Bulgarian Armenians, who in most cases do not master this alphabet but still try to acquire it, each in their own way. By seeing how the symbols of the alphabet, Mount Ararat, the pomegranate, and the Armenian refugee impact the collective Armenian consciousness, serving as elements of identification and permeating the imagery about the "Motherland," I became more aware of how I myself have been influenced and continue to be influenced by them in my research. In this context, it is impossible to ignore the necessary symbolic dimension (Krasteva 1999) that permeates the lives of this ethnic minority in a special, emotional, and all-encompassing way.

This has led me to analyze the dynamics by which a minority group can manage to survive in space and time and to see this in connection with the very particular way in which I have managed to nurture within myself the memory of my being Armenian. Therefore, I believe that the Armenian alphabet, in particular, viewed more broadly as a "cultural tradition of writing," in conjunction with the memory of the Genocide suffered by this people, is the key element for Armenians that can tie together all the dots of the initial question. This is the basis from which to start, but it stands in a non-exclusive relationship with other key elements that are essential for defining the most complete picture of the situation: seen in this way, the importance of the alphabet coexists with its lack of practical knowledge by part of the community and also by me.

This book thus focuses on the symbolic aspect of Armenian diaspora identity and identifies the mechanisms of its persistence over time as a social and cultural construct based on a traditionalist view on Armenian collectivity. At the same time, it aims to highlight the specific "transnational" or "transcending" (Bjorklund 2003) attributes that make the Armenian diaspora an extremely complex and multi-layered phenomenon in terms of affiliations, imaginaries, and agencies, which evolve in individual, symbolic forms of "Armenianness," viewed as a more personal choice of expressing one's sense of belonging (Bakalian 1993: 6–7).

In determining how much the past is used ideologically to foster social cohesion (Eriksen 2001: 272), the use of the alphabet is not to be understood only in terms of the practical way in which it is employed by people in order to transcribe the sounds of the Armenian language, but rather as a symbolic modality in which it becomes part of a process of identity cultivation encouraged by the educated elite of the community and its traditionalist perception of identity. According to the ideology spread by the intelligentsia, Armenians have historically become a "nation" only after the creation of their own alphabet. Therefore, we can trace a sort of "ethnogenic" rhetoric on the alphabet, which is carried out in different public settings with the purpose of feeding collective consciousness and promoting internal cohesion within the diasporic community of Plovdiv. As a consequence, we observe how Saint Mesrop Mashtots, (the creator of the Armenian alphabet), his translation activity, the old manuscripts, etc. are living elements, resignified in their present role as symbols of the history of Armenian written culture development that continues to produce meaningful values even in the micro-context of a diasporic community such as that of Plovdiv.

This volume is divided as follows: In the first section, I introduce the subject and aims of the book, presenting the theoretical frameworks and addressing the methodological aspects of this study. Chapter 2 deals with the historical contextualization of the Armenian diaspora of Plovdiv from its origins to the present. Chapter 3 focuses on the symbolic function played by language in the Armenian diaspora, examining, in particular, the value acquired by its graphic aspect as a marker of cultural distinctiveness and as an element that supports collective cohesion and remembrance practices. Chapter 4 deals with the school domain and examines the symbols, narratives, and ideologies conveyed to children attending the local Armenian school and the Saturday classes. Chapter 5 focuses on the role of the international diaspora organization, AGBU ("Armenian General Benevolent Union"/Parekordzagan) in promoting positive linguistic attitudes and collective memory practices (in particular, on the Genocide) through both print media and social activities. Chapter 6 deals with Armenian literature published in Plovdiv, with special attention to Suren Vetsigian's memoir on the Genocide and on the book of Armenian cuisine. Chapter 7 examines the identifying function of written language and memory in various sites that make up the "linguistic landscape" of the city of Plovdiv, looking at examples of public writing appearing on monuments, graves, and other spaces. Chapter 8 problematizes the issues of diaspora belongings by examining the memory and mobility practices with the "lost" homeland in Turkey and the relationship with the current Republic of Armenia. It also summarizes the main findings of this research in relation to the processes of symbolic cultivation in the diaspora, with attention to the "native" Armenian alphabet.

Foreword by Boghos Levon Zekiyan

I welcome with great pleasure the invitation from Giustina Selvelli, my former student at Ca' Foscari University of Venice, to write down a few words to present her book *Language Attitudes, Collective Memory and (Trans) National Identity Construction among the Armenian Diaspora in Bulgaria.*

It is not only a pleasure but also an honor for me to undertake this task. It means that many seeds sown during those intensive hours of lessons have not only borne fruit in the inner spaces of the soul but have also reached the dimension of scholarly research and production. Selvelli's work is remarkable for a number of reasons.

First, it is related to an Armenian community that is, of course, part of the modern great Armenian diaspora. But it reflects at the same time, as Selvelli's research proves with scientific precision, and also in a fascinating way, the profoundly communitarian dimension of this Armenian settlement in a very special corner of Bulgaria. This community is the bearer of historical evocations and memories, almost a small laboratory of re-enactments, a model also for today's much more anonymous diasporic units that have formed after the Armenian Genocide in the various corners of the great Western world, from Europe to America and Australia, with their main centers in large metropolises like Paris, Boston, New York, and later Los Angeles, or in smaller urban realities like Watertown, MA, in the USA.

Second, Plovdiv offers a model in which the communitarian identity of the group enjoys somehow a de facto "official" recognition in the mental attitudes and behavior of the local population, which to some extent influences the attitudes of public authorities, a fact which can to some extent be interpreted as a legacy of the Ottoman state system in recognizing non-Muslim non-territorial minorities.

It is interesting to observe how the decision of the communist regime in Bulgaria to close the school of the Armenian community dealt a heavy blow to the survival of the knowledge and practice of the Armenian language in the younger generations of the Armenian community. This was an irony of fate, as communist regimes often acted as strongly nationalistic state systems and proved to be opponents of communitarian or minoritarian entities. In the absence of the democratic principle of recognizing private schools like other private activities, there was no longer room for the Armenian community of Plovdiv, which for many reasons, both historical and sociological, could provide an effective model of a non-territorial minority in an Eastern European context, similar to the Armenian communities in Middle Eastern countries. These act, or rather acted, with a remarkable social, educational, and ecclesiastical organization before the massive weakening of Armenianness, which today is almost on the verge of extinction due to the catastrophic political situation of the last decades in these countries, especially in Lebanon and Syria.

Many considerations, thoughts, and reflections can be developed from other insightful suggestions, and events of particular interest mentioned and analyzed by Selvelli.

These, apart from their theoretical weight, can certainly be of great help to face, in a more rational and humanly acceptable way, the great adventure of mass emigrations that we are witnessing today and that, unfortunately, we often deal with, even in unworthy ways.

I take the opportunity to congratulate Dr. Giustina Selvelli and to wish her a fruitful scholarly activity and public engagement in the field of the rights and policies concerning minorities, especially non-territorial ones, which are among the most vital issues and most decisive challenges of our days.

Boghos Levon Zekiyan
Venice – Istanbul, March 24, 2023

Acknowledgments

The publication of this book has been made possible thanks to the generous funding provided by the Foundation Calouste Gulbenkian to whom I cannot express enough gratitude.

This research would not have taken place without the help, support, and friendship of a great number of Armenians of Plovdiv who welcomed me in their community from the very beginning since early 2010: first of all, Mrs. Malvina Manoukyan, the tireless teacher and educator whose courses allowed me to understand the nature of love for the Armenian language. Her premature death in summer 2012 was a shock to me as it was for this community. I will always be thankful to Mr. Rupen Chavushyan, the head of the local AGBU/*Parekordzagan* branch, who provided me with the most important information on the social spaces and activities of the community and always found the time to answer to my numerous questions.

I am grateful to Hripsime Erniasyan for the valuable information on the written culture and publications in Plovdiv, for sending me the AGBU bulletin and books to Italy throughout all these years, and for welcoming me in the editorial offices during each visit to Plovdiv and not letting me out of it without valuable materials as presents. Mrs. Srpuhi, who became a kind of adoptive grandmother for me during my first fieldwork in 2010, with whom I regularly attended Church liturgy every Sunday and the meetings at the pensioners' club on Tuesdays. A big thanks go to my dear friend Nora Radoslavova and her mother Lusona Cherchiayan, who were among the most precious sources of information on the community since the beginning and made me feel welcomed in their home as a part of their family, Viržinija Garabedyan for her kindness and availability when she was an Armenian school director, Gayane Shahugyan, Aneta and Silva Zyumyurtyan, Suzana H. and her husband; poet and writer Hovannes Mikaelyan (Oncho) for his time and written works and his friend Sarkis, Ahavni Kevorkyan for her time and emotional conversations, and many other people who contributed to make me feel connected and part of their community life.

I am grateful to the Professors at the Department of Ethnology of the Paisii Hilendarski University of Plovdiv: Professor Stoyan Antonov, in whose course on ethnic minorities I was familiarized with the fundamental concepts of "ethnosymbolism," Professor Maria Schnitter, who always helped me getting in touch with ethnic minority representatives.

I also want to thank the professors who supported my research and study during the years of my MA studies at Ca' Foscari University of Venice: Professor Boghos Levon Zekiyan, for introducing me to Armenian studies and providing the essential tools to navigate its complex culture and language; Professor Sona Haroutyunian, for her amazing classes of Armenian language; Professor Aldo Ferrari, who introduced me to the study of Armenian diaspora communities in Europe and beyond; Professor Glauco Sanga, who made me discover the crucial field of the Anthropology of Writing and the studies of Giorgio Raimondo Cardona; and Professor Iliyana Krapova, who supported in many ways my various periods of mobility to the beautiful city of Plovdiv. I am also grateful to AGBU and its Armenian Virtual College for allowing me to improve my knowledge of the Armenian language, thanks to their free online courses of Western Armenian.

Contents

1. Introduction: Symbols and Memory in the Armenian Diaspora

Abstract: In this first section, I introduce the subject and aims of the book, focusing on its theoretical foundations, and explaining the role of symbols in the construction of collective identity, as well as the importance of written culture for Armenian communities. I also address the methodological aspects of this study and reconstruct the details of my ethnographic fieldwork with the community.

Keywords: symbolic cultivation, Armenian alphabet, Armenian diaspora, ethnographic fieldwork, ethnic memory

1.1. Overview of the Topic

The aim of this work is to examine, through an anthropological and ethnographic approach, the promotion of Armenian identity in the diasporic context of the Bulgarian city of Plovdiv through the use of specific symbols (above all the autochthonous alphabet) and memory practices (in particular the narratives related to the Genocide and the lost homeland) by the local Armenian intelligentsia. The Armenian language and its writing system are considered here not only in terms of the practical way in which people use them to communicate (speaking, reading, and writing) but primarily as fundamental tools in a process of "symbolic cultivation" (Smith 2009) of collective identity. This process is sustained, among other things, by the rhetoric according to which Armenians have historically become a nation only after the creation of their alphabet, a discourse disseminated in various social domains to cultivate collective memory practices and to foster internal cohesion within this Armenian diaspora community.

My research on the Armenians in this Bulgarian city demonstrates that language and the alphabet play a primary function in practices of collective self-representation, being used by local elites to engage audiences in a discourse of ethnic identity. Involvement is reinforced by the strong cultural, symbolic, and emotional content of these elements, which are charged with an additional rhetoric of the "survival" of the Armenian people in connection with the memory of the Genocide perpetrated by the Ottoman authorities against their ancestors. These elements are part of a cultural system that involves an ideological use of the past (Eriksen 2001: 272, Zerubavel 2004) and by which ethnic identity perpetuates itself. This is done through inherited cultural representations, defined as "ethnic memory" (Fabietti 2004: 145) consisting of symbols that remind people of their common belonging. In order to be constitutive of ethnic memory, such symbols must be "remembered" through repetitions or actualizations associated with a specific culture of memory. This, in turn, is very often conveyed precisely by various forms of writing, understood in terms of textual production not only as literature, journalism, and poetry but also as public examples of inscription of communal space through monuments, gravestones, and memorial plaques. Language and writing are thus linked to the ethnic question insofar as they prove to be tools, but also objects of cultural memory, here understood as an attribution of meaning realized through explicit reference to symbols, rituals, and myths (Cohen 1985) as founding elements of collective belonging, or an "imagined community" (Anderson 1991).

If we look at the use of writing in Western societies, we find that it has almost exclusively a communicative function, serving the transmission of information; however, in other societies, writing systems can also play a role in other areas of social life, for example, as a decorative and monumental element: the example of calligraphy is surely an eloquent one (Cardona 2009: 171). Writing can thus take on new functions, as in the case of Armenians in the diaspora, where its role is also to convey various meanings of highly symbolic nature. Such reasons make writing a suitable subject for anthropological investigation: it was created by people and is culturally transmitted. It has both symbolic value and material aspects; it is crucial for interaction between people and central to the creation of knowledge that is passed intergenerationally (Barton & Papen 2010: 4).

In the Armenian case, apart from being inextricably linked to the religious and spiritual dimension (as in the case of Arabic), the unique script created by Mesrop Mashtots in 405 A.D. also became a crucial element of national identity, enriched with an "ethnogenic" content. Indeed, the origin of the alphabet is viewed by Armenians as coinciding with that of the people who started making use of it, and through its characters the strength of a legendary invention is propagated across generations. The alphabet is thus treated through identity rhetoric spread by "cultural elites" as the true bond of ethnic intimacy and as the cornerstone of the nation, in many ways as a revealing element of "authentic" collective experience.

Italian linguist Giorgio Raimondo Cardona (1982: 5) claims that, by virtue of its indirect contact with thought, writing can acquire some of the power contained in it: propositional, active, creative, depending on the ideologies behind it. In the case of Armenians, the stronger ideology is the one related to the memory of the past or the exercise of an "ethnic memory," so we can claim that the main function attributed to the written word is the one evocative of ethnicity and distinctiveness.

In the history of its distance from the motherland, Armenian identity has expressed itself not only through the subjective dimension of affection, memory, and imagery (Zekiyan 2000: 168) but also as an objective entity in a social reality that makes use of written records in the broadest sense. Against this background, I have analyzed how the element of writing—that is, the graphic aspect of the Armenian language, becomes embedded in the collective consciousness of the community through its employment as a recurrent motif in written production; in education through learning exercises and the "ethnohistory" (Barth 1998: 12) it carries on, and in the physical space of the community (on monuments, plaques, etc.) for commemoration purposes. In all these cases, the Armenian writing system stands out as the main cultural marker for the city's Armenian community, rooted in discourses on the ethical imperative of remembering the suffering of Armenians in the 1890s (with the "Hamidian massacres") and especially the Genocide against them in the years of World War I.

The fundamental question for me was to understand how it was possible for the Armenian people, scattered throughout history to all parts of the world, to preserve forms of collective (national) consciousness despite the absence of an independent homeland (until 30 years ago), and the assimilation tendencies of the various powers to which they were subjected.

Thus, my hypothesis of the importance of the Armenian language and its "protective" graphic aspect, that is, the autochthonous alphabet, gradually prevailed and combined with a perceived need for an explanation related to the symbolic cultivation of the collective imagination. In this view, the study of ethnicity as an operative group is complemented by the study of the representational factors that enable this group to exist within the symbolic horizon of its members. In this respect, it is important to emphasize that a distinct language and written tradition represent important areas for the maintenance of many nations through authentic ethnic traditions: this is especially true for peoples who possessed their own distinctive alphabet, such as the Armenians and Georgians, who have been historically defined as ethnolinguistic communities (Smith 2007: 328).

In the Armenian diaspora, like the one in Plovdiv, important socially active players such as diaspora organizations, educated elites, and the Armenian Apostolic Church contribute to the promotion of a specific language ideology that opposes assimilation and praises knowledge of the Armenian language: this is embedded in a discourse on ethnic identity and community survival in the context of globalization, which also proves crucial for improving the minority's relations with the Republic of Armenia and the world diaspora. According to this perspective, ethnolinguistic minorities can survive for a long time without political autonomy or their own territory, but social and cultural factors must compensate for the absence of such elements (Smith 1992: 439). For the current Armenian diaspora, the most significant factors in this respect are the memory practices related to the trauma of Genocide and the loss of the homeland (Kasbarian 2015: 359), as well as the cult of the mother tongue (and its writing system) connecting to the ancestral heritage. In the Armenian diaspora, the intimacy and sense of authenticity created by the linguistic bond are linked to its ability to form a symbolic boundary (Barth 1998: 34) against assimilation, and this is reinforced by the unique and distinctive graphic system, that is, the Armenian alphabet, created uniquely for this language by St. Mesrop Mashtots in the early 5th century (Maksoudian 2006: 157), which made him "almost the cornerstone of the historical consciousness of the Armenian identity" (Zekiyan 2000: 181).

To penetrate the symbolic world of a community, it is essential to become familiar with its shared memories and beliefs, and to analyze how they are perpetuated by the sociocultural activities of a particular intelligentsia. In addition, we need to assess the continuing impact of ethnic myths, symbols, and traditions on the consciousness of the people and how they continue to influence current behaviors and attitudes. Clearly, ethnic ideologies depend on cultural "raw material" as a starting point, but this is reworked and used in particular ways so that ethnicity results from a combination of symbolic and social or political dimensions (Eriksen 2001: 275). The key terms here are "selection" and "resonance" (Smith 2009: 31–2): the category of nation is indeed based on a carefully selected range of cultural values referring to the history of its people. Among Armenians, the belief of being a "chosen people" (Smith 1992: 444) is a not-insignificant factor in the preservation of their culture. Pride in being the first nation in the world to embrace Christianity, combined with pride in their script, solidified their belief in ethnic election and divine mission. The alphabet has the function of a symbol of distinctiveness, and the story of its creation carries forward an ethnic myth of divine inspiration.

The ethno-symbolist approach of historical sociologist Anthony D. Smith argues that cultural elements such as symbols, myths, and memories are as much a part of a people's social reality as any other material or organizational factor (Smith 2009: 25): indeed, social reality is inconceivable without symbolism. However, he also stresses how wrong it is to consider the "symbolic" as something purely externally constructed, since its specificity lies precisely in the fact that it resonates to a great extent with the inner world of people. This is why educated elites constructing the national discourse use these elements to achieve emotional involvement among community members. Symbols and myths ensure a degree of collective consciousness- if not cohesion- in times of crisis and change by providing the community with a symbolic repertoire that helps it distinguish itself from other similar communities in the eyes of its members and outsiders. At the same time, this shared symbolic tradition continues to define the community and ensure a sense of continuity with previous generations.

It has been said that in every society, a series of memory sites exist, which correspond to places of commemorative record and practice where "remembrance anchors the past" (Linke 2005). These are categorized as "topographical places (archives, libraries, museums); monumental places (cemeteries, architectural edifices); symbolic places (commemorative rites, pilgrimages, emblems); functional places (manuals, autobiographies, associations); and places of power (states, elites, milieux)" (Linke 2005). In line with this classification, in this book all these categories are considered: for example, as topographical places the "small museum" of the Genocide in the Plovdiv church crypt; as monumental places, among others, the town's cemetery and its monuments recalling the collective tragedy; as symbolic places, the residents' marches in commemoration of the Genocide and the trips to the historical Armenian cities and towns in today's Turkey; and as functional places, the activities and publications (periodical press and books) of the Armenian General Benevolent Union (AGBU)/ Parekordzagan, the main diaspora organization worldwide. As for the places of power, I will highlight the role of the AGBU/Parekordzagan as the main philanthropic, cultural, and political organ of the Armenian diaspora in Bulgaria.

1.2. Anthropological Approaches to Writing Practices and Writing Systems

"The anthropologist is above all interested in unwritten data, not so much because the people he studies are incapable of writing, but because that with which he is principally concerned differs from everything men ordinarily think of recording on stone or on paper" (Strauss 1963: 25). This sentence was written by anthropologist Claude Lévi-Strauss at a time when anthropology had little interest in the study of writing and written texts (De Certeau 2005: 30). The discipline's eyes were firmly fixed on the "exotic" and the culturally other (Barton & Papen 2010: 5), and in most cases this "Other" was a society that did not rely on writing for communication. Thus, oral cultures were predominantly studied, and writing was a cultural trait that belonged exclusively to the anthropologist/outsider. In contemporary anthropology, much of this has changed, and a crucial turning point was Clifford and Marcus' 1986 work *Writing Culture*, in which they firmly stated the necessity to pay more attention to the written texts and testimonies produced by the people anthropologists do research on. My approach was inspired by the principle that it is no longer possible to work as if the outside researcher is the sole or primary author: it is important to consider the role of co-authors, that is, the fact that informants have the opportunity to interpret what has been and is being written about their culture. That is why an important role in this book is played by the written testimonies produced by the Armenian diaspora in Plovdiv, being these novels, poems, newspaper articles, but also examples of public writing in the spaces of the community.

The encounter with the theories of the great Italian scholar Giorgio Raimondo Cardona (1981, 1982, 1986) was fundamental for my development of an anthropological approach to issues related to writing systems and writing practices. Cardona was the first to establish the field of the anthropology of writing, departing from the assumption that the cultural significance of writing goes far beyond its technical function. This allowed a new level of interpretation of writing that revealed a profound symbolic aspect linked to (personal and collective) cultural identity practices. Furthermore, this "extralinguistic" interpretation (Fishman 1977: XII) of writing systems stood in opposition to the old notions expressed by linguists and semiologists, such as De Saussure, who attributed no specific or autonomous value to the graphic form of the language and wrote that "[l]anguage and writing are two distinct systems of signs; the second exists for the sole purpose of representing the first. The linguistic object is not both the written and the spoken forms of words; the spoken forms alone constitute the object" (De Saussure 1959: 23). In this sense, an anthropological perspective means examining the production of writing as a cultural and social practice: written texts are central to culture in its broadest sense (Barton & Papen 2010: 9). On this premise, we can also better understand what writing means to a community: it reveals much about the people who use it and their cultural world. Above all, writing is a privileged site of symbolic production and becomes an effective means of "remembering" who one is: the Armenian case fully expresses this.

In this context, emphasis is placed on the producers of written culture and on the ways they engage in broader social practices perpetuating specific ideological discourses of collective identity. Of critical importance, therefore, is the role of individuals and institutions that support literacy practices, as well as specific views on the nature of reading and writing. It is also important to remark that the notion of a division between literate and illiterate people is not pertinent in relation to such processes: within the Armenian community, even people who cannot read and write in the community language or have low literacy skills participate in complex literacy practices. Thus, written texts are used not only by those capable of deciphering them.

The nationalism that began to develop from 1800 undoubtedly relied on Herder's assertion that language was the spirit of a people, which reinforced the equation of language and ethnicity; however, this link between identity and language is not just a romantic concept. Language had already played a politically significant role before the French Revolution, and examples such as the Armenian and Georgian nations prove this (Smith 1991: 38). It is no coincidence that both nations possess a unique and distinctive alphabet, which they have preserved over centuries. Although nationalism is a modern phenomenon, in some cases already rooted communities or ethnicities did show a sense of community comparable to the "national" before the emergence of nation-states (Dufoix 2008: 15). With regard to Armenians, the long and well-documented historical tradition of this people cannot be put on the same level of nationalities that emerged only in the modern times or have only recently become self-aware. Nevertheless, continuity does not mean immobility (Ferrari 2003: 110), since ethnic identity should be viewed as an aspect of a relationship and not as a property of a person or group (Barth 1998: 15). This relational interpretation of ethnic identity also presupposes that the existence of an ethnic group is socially and ideologically validated by the recognition among members and outsiders alike that it is culturally different (Chai 2005: 375).

The historical issue of the relationship with other sociocultural groups was a crucial element in the creation of Armenian identity, especially during the period of adoption of an autochthonous script and subsequent derivation of Monophysite Christianity. In order to survive as a distinct people and not be assimilated, Armenians thus resorted to markers of cultural difference. The same dynamic is currently taking place in the diaspora and continues to require the activation of practical and symbolic resources often associated with the field of writing.

1.3. The Armenian Diaspora: Conceptualizing Transnational Belongings

When we refer to a diaspora, we usually mean a community of people who live permanently outside their real or imaginary homeland. The word "diaspora" is etymologically derived from the Greek verb *diaspéiro*, "to disperse": the word itself contains the idea of an original place from which the dispersion took place and evokes images of a journey of people who have a distinct collective memory and nourish a myth of return (Panossian 1998: 150). The concept of diaspora is a complex one (Brubaker 2005), since it underscores the continuing relationship of people to their (imaginary) homeland in relation to the construction of complex patterns of non-exclusive, transnational, or translocal belonging (Levitt Schiller 2004: 1011). The word, associated above all with the fate of Armenians and Jews, has acquired a traumatic connotation, that of a people driven from their territory and whose numbers outside the borders of the homeland exceed those within it.

The diaspora (*spyurk* in Armenian, meaning "dispersed people") is a condition currently shared by 9 to 10 million Armenians around the world, according to the 2019 estimates (Vardanyan 2021: 48). Less than 3 million is instead the population of the Republic of Armenia, which has diminished over the course of the last 20 years. Dispersion in Armenian history has been the result of destabilizing factors that have affected the Armenian homeland since ancient times, including political instability, conquest, religious persecution, massacres, and deportation.

Boghos Levon Zekiyan (2000: 143) recalls that, strictly speaking, the Armenians who fled the Ottoman Empire did not become a diaspora until the independent Republic of Armenia began to exist.[1] The situations that arose after the collapse of Greater Armenia (1045) and the Kingdom of Cilicia (1375) are not yet true diasporas as a result of Genocide and forced displacement from their homeland, but rather can be described as "colonies." Emigration from their historical homeland was also voluntary, in search of opportunities for foreign trade, education, and military careers (Aslanian 2011).

Armenians have long been established in hundreds of communities and colonies throughout the world. Their migration has been continuous

---

[1] See Boghos Levon Zekiyan: "In our opinion, we can only talk of a diaspora in the strict sense, that is, a state of 'dispersion,' starting with the aftermath of the 1915 massacre (…) For the period prior to 1915 it would be more appropriate to talk about 'colonies' (…) A large part of the Armenian people still lived on their territories." Author's translation – G. S.

throughout history (Ivančev 2005), although relatively intense migrations can be noted, especially to the areas of interest to this study, particularly to the Balkan Peninsula during the Byzantine period between the 7th and 11th centuries. Beginning in the first half of the 11th century, cooperation between the Armenians and Byzantium broke down, and the empire forced the Armenian dynasties to cede their kingdoms in exchange for land in Eastern Cappadocia and Cilicia (Ferrari 2003: 26). This event greatly intensified the processes of emigration, and a dispersion of this people began, by which the Armenians passed beyond the Mediterranean to India and Tibet, Ethiopia, and Russia.

> Historical events presented the Armenian people with a challenge whose response led to a remarkable anthropological transformation. The abandonment of traditional activities in favor of trade and finance, which later made Armenians famous all over the world, was thus a vital and energetic response to the forced uprooting from the ancestral territory and the need to adapt to diasporic reality. (Ferrari 2003: 29, my translation)

This model of "differentiated integration" (Zekiyan 2013: 90–95), adopted by Armenian diaspora communities around the world and which would become prevalent from 1600 onward as their trading activities developed, allowed for the maintenance of national and cultural identity without ghettoization or discrimination (Ferrari 2003: 30). Even today, the sociocultural elites of the Armenian diaspora continue to promote the affirmation of a constant will not to be assimilated (Van Hear 1998: 55), which is implemented through practices of self-representation in order to distinguish a specific "Armenian identity" from that of the majority in the host country. This need for cultural distinctiveness is also achieved through the use of a particular rhetoric of unity.

In examining the long-term persistence of ethnic groups in a translocal perspective, a key element is certainly the way in which the construction of collective cultural units based on common ancestry, shared memories, and symbols is made possible (Smith 1992: 437). Ethnic communities can survive for a long time without political autonomy, without their own territory, but social, cultural, and psychological factors must compensate for the absence of such elements. This suggests that we need to pay more attention to the subjective components in the survival of ethnic groups (Smith 2009: 25ff). In addition, it is important to point out that the "survival" of ethnic groups depends primarily on the work of specialists who actively cultivate a high degree of distinctiveness and a collective mission. Members of an ethnic community must feel that they possess irreplaceable cultural values and that their heritage must be preserved through the identification of its members with certain enduring memories, symbols, and traditions (Smith 1992: 439). As has been noted (Fabietti 2004: 148), ethnic survival does not require the maintenance of an intact culture or even a motherland, as the Armenian and Jewish examples show, but rather the exercise of a particular memory. Indeed, this leads to a symbolic transfiguration of elements that are significant for the production and reproduction of ethnocultural identity.

1.4. Methodology

My research has aimed to embrace different fields of study, namely the anthropology of writing, ethnic minority studies, and collective memory studies; the anthropology of diaspora; and as well as, to a small extent, the sociolinguistics of endangered languages.[2] The Armenian language, in fact, while not endangered in today's Republic of Armenia, is at risk of extinction in its Western variant as a minority language in Bulgaria and other countries of the global diaspora.

My first contact with the Armenian diaspora of Plovdiv dates back to 2010 when I spent one year of fieldwork with the community as I prepared my Master's thesis. Initially, I devoted myself to observing language education for children by attending Armenian classes at the Tutunjyan Armenian School for about three months and also participating in the so-called "Saturday School." In this educational context, I had the opportunity to hold numerous conversations and interviews with the three Armenian language teachers at the time, one of whom also volunteered to teach the Saturday School classes. I also met with

---

2   This field of study, which I was introduced to through a summer course organized in the summer of 2009 by the SOAS University of London in collaboration with the Hans Rausing Endangered Languages Project, made me realize that my sensitivity to ethnic minority issues could be combined in a practical way with the study of the dynamics of preserving their linguistic diversity.

the directors of the school, talked with some parents, and of course had conversations with the children. Participating in Armenian classes allowed me to understand the conditions that enable children to acquire literacy skills in a different and difficult graphic system whose practical usefulness in daily life is rather limited. Moreover, I was able to discover the symbolic dimension of identity in the teachers' teaching and in their rhetoric of identity.

In addition, I then analyzed the written production in the local media, especially the biweekly *Parekordzagani Tzain*, the weekly *Vahan*, the magazine *Menk*—all of which were in Bulgarian and Armenian—and the books published by the local publishers *Armen Tur* and *Parekordzagan*. The last part of my research was based on the continuous observation of the public spaces where the Armenian alphabet can be found: the courtyard of the Armenian community, with its walls and its monuments and objects, the cemetery, the school, the collection in the crypt of the church, and any other place important for the community. My fieldwork activities were also characterized by the observation of and participation in most of the religious, cultural, and social events of the Armenian community: liturgy of the Apostolic and Evangelical Churches, celebrations of important holidays and anniversaries in the Cultural Center, theater performances, book presentations, student evenings, dinners of the Erevan Association and AGBU, meetings in the Pensioners' Club, as well as numerous visits to newspaper offices and people who opened their doors, invited me to lunch or dinner, and shared their memories and thoughts with me.

Thanks to my frequent visits to the city after 2010, to my personal and professional relations with various members of the community, and the continuous reading of their publications, I was able to continue my research on the Armenians of Plovdiv throughout all these years.

In all, I was able to conduct about fifty individual and, in some cases, group interviews with a wide range of people from the community, varying in gender, age (roughly from 6 to 80), professional background, etc. The interviews were free-flowing and not rigidly structured but in all respects attempted to touch on topics related to the alphabet, literacy practices, the memory of the ancestors and the "post-memory" (Hirsch 2008) of the Genocide, and personal connection to the Armenian homeland and the diaspora. A large part of the interviews was conducted with school personnel, journalists, writers and poets, and others who make up the so-called Armenian "intelligentsia" of the city, as well as with students, parents, and members of local associations.

2. History of the Armenian Diaspora of Plovdiv

Abstract: This chapter deals with the historical contextualization of the Armenian diaspora of Plovdiv from its origins to the present. It also reconstructs the different phases of this community in terms of language use and printing activities, paying particular attention to the arrival of Armenian refugees between the late 19th century and the aftermath of World War I, the conditions during communism, and the perspectives since the post-socialist phase of transition.

Keywords: Paulicians, Armenian refugees, Armenian Genocide, Armenians under communism, Armenians and post-socialism

2.1. Armenian Communities from Byzantine to Ottoman Times

The Armenians are one of the oldest communities to have settled in Bulgaria: it is believed that the first Armenians arrived here as early as the 5th century (Markov 2001: 23), before the proto-Bulgarian peoples and the Slavs, although there is no written evidence from that period. Instead, all Byzantine chroniclers from the beginning of the 7th century to the 11th century mention the forcible deportation of the Armenian population composed of Paulicians and Orthodox Apostolics, to the territory of present-day Bulgaria (Papazian-Tanielian 2016: 193–194).

A massive wave of migration took place under the Byzantine Emperor Constantine V, who deported whole masses of Armenians in 741–745 to prevent the spread of the Paulician heresy in the Asian territories belonging to the Empire (Tavitian 2021: 38ff). The heretics were resettled in distant Thrace, in the area of the then city of Philippopolis, which bordered the distant and feared Bulgarian Empire (Arnaudov 2001: 211). After the Christianization of Bulgaria occurred in 864,[3] other Paulicians penetrated

---

3   One fact to remember is that Cyril and Methodius, the inventors of the Glagolitic Slavonic alphabet, in their papal mission to Italy had brought as an argument

the country and helped sow the seeds of future Bogomilism. Paulicianism was a dualistic heresy that had developed in the Armenian territories and on the Eastern borders of the Byzantine Empire, in areas that were in contact with the Iranian Mazdaic religion, which was considered a threat to the stability of the Empire (Hamilton & Hamilton 1998).

The normalization policy of the Byzantine emperors received a new impetus under John Tsimiskes (969–976), who in turn settled a large number of heretics in Philippopolis to create a militarized strip of territory for protection against incursions from the north. He cracked down on the Armenian Paulicians, as they constituted a sect and were seen as destroying the unity of the Church and the Empire. However, according to Armenian sources, the heretics were joined by Christians who belonged to the Apostolic Church.

The Paulicians soon proved unreliable, however, as they allied themselves with the Bulgarians, who were the Byzantines' most feared enemy after the Persians. The disturbing Armenian presence in the vicinity of the Thracian capital is explicitly handed down to us by Anna Comnena, the daughter of Emperor Alexius:

> [Philippopolis] consists of three hills, [...] There were several ways in which [the city] was unfortunate, but especially in the presence there of many impious people. For the Armenians had taken possession of this city, together with those called Bogomils, about whom and about their heresy I shall speak when it is appropriate, as well as the most impious Paulicians. (Hamilton & Hamilton 1998: 169)

By the end of the 12th century, both the Paulicians and the Monophysite Armenians, together with the Bulgarian population, participated in the struggles to liberate the regions of Thrace and Macedonia from Byzantine rule and to unite them with the Bulgarian Empire. Paulicianism did not end here, however, but contributed significantly to the development of the Bogomil heresy, which arose shortly thereafter and had a large following among the Bosnian population (Aslanian 1993: 71–75).

---

against the restriction of three Biblical the example of the Armenians who had long since possessed their own alphabet, their own literature, and conducted the church liturgy in their mother tongue. See also: Markov 2001: 25.

In the 12th and 13th centuries, there were large Armenian colonies not only in Plovdiv, Sofia, and Tarnovo but also in many other cities in the Bulgarian-Macedonian area.

The next major phase of Armenian settlement in Bulgaria occurred in the period after the fall of Constantinople in 1453. In the 15th century, one of the great Armenian physicians of the late Middle Ages, Amirdovlat from Amasia, a city in Asia Minor, spent part of his life in Filibe (the Ottoman name Plovdiv). He lived here for almost 10 years and from 1466 to 1469 wrote his work "The Benefit of Medicine," his main work on clinical medicine. In his correspondence he mentions the names of the patients he treated—Bulgarians, Turks, Greeks, and Armenians, from which it can be concluded that Armenians lived in Plovdiv at that time (Artanyan 2000: 8). The following most intense wave of Armenian migration to this city dates back to the time of Ottoman Sultan Mehmed IV from the newly conquered territories of Poland (Artanyan 2000: 9). During the invasion of Poland, some Armenian communities living there moved to the Bulgarian territories, first to the Black Sea coast and then to Plovdiv. In this city they settled permanently in 1672, thanks to the support of an Armenian merchant named Abro Çelebi, who was so influential with the Turkish authorities that he obtained permission from the Sultan to house all the refugees from Poland here (Giligyan 2002). In 1675, Armenians in Ottoman Plovdiv obtained the right to their first church by receiving one of the eight Greek Orthodox churches, renamed from "Agios Giorgos" to "Surp Kevork" (which means the same in Armenian). The Church was given to the Armenians by the Sultan,[4] again through the intercession of merchant Abro Çelebi.

As for the diaspora within the Ottoman Empire, the concept of community, identity, and organization was derived from the *millet* system, an example of pre-modern religious pluralism (Castellan 1991: 133–138). The *millet*'s distinguishing criterion was religion: it was a community embedded in a larger polity, with some degree of self-government, quasi-autonomous structures, and some forms of legitimate representation (Manoukian

---

4   The Sultan's firman that authorized the construction is now hung in the church museum.

1986: 78), held together by pre-modern political ideals. The stronghold of the Armenian *millet* (the *ermeni millet*) was the Church, which represented a kind of symbol and definition of community identity: a kind of substitute for the Armenian state, which did not exist.[5] In the period around the turn of the 17th and 18th centuries, a real Armenian quarter was formed in the vicinity of the church, in Plovdiv where also the new groups of Armenians settled, who kept arriving in the next two centuries. After their arrival in Bulgaria, the Armenians established their own enterprises for processing tobacco, leather, and silk. They also mastered watchmaking, goldsmithing, carpentry, and jewelry making, as well as medicine (Ivanova 2008: 12).

During the Ottoman period, sizable Armenian communities lived in Plovdiv, Sofia, Dobrič, Varna, Silistra, Burgas, Razgrad, and Šumen. In Plovdiv, an Armenian school was founded in 1834. As mentioned, the *millet* system provided that certain ethno-religious communities had a recognized status, so they could organize and self-manage with a wide margin of freedom: in this context, education in the mother tongue was legally permitted and there were, indeed, many Armenian schools throughout the Ottoman Empire. In those same years, the house of prominent merchant Stepan Hindliyan[6] was built. In 1846 followed the construction of the house of Krikor Mesrobovič, a wealthy landowner and moneylender who was a close friend of Stepan Hindliyan. Both buildings today represent one of the most important museums in the Old Town and are located in the former historic Armenian quarter, where the Armenian community of that time lived relatively compactly, a fact recorded, for example, in the plan of the city of Filibe by G. Lejean from 1867 (Lejean 1867).

---

5   Under pressure from European powers and during the Tanzimat restructuring period (1839–76), decrees such as the Hatt-ı Şerif of Gülhane (1839) and the Imperial Reform Edict, or Islâhat Firmân (1956), were issued that guaranteed the existence and rights of Christians (Castellan 1991: 311). After the 1856 Reform Edict, each non-Muslim community was authorized to establish a statute on the administration of its internal affairs (Voillery 2012: 190). However, injustices continued, while at the same time internal and international tensions were exacerbated by the military and economic decline of the empire.

6   He reached as far as India, and this earned him the surname "Hindliyan".

The 1870s were the period of the so-called Bulgarian Renaissance (or Bulgarian National Revival), marked by the fights for liberation from Ottoman rule. Bulgarian Armenians actively participated in the struggle, side by side with Bulgarians, providing them with weapons from Constantinople, Bursa, and Smyrna (Iliev 2001: 362).

During these years, some Bulgarian revolutionaries were exiled by the Ottoman authorities to the city of Diyarbakır in Southeastern Anatolia, where they found the support of the Armenian communities living there. Through the influence of these Bulgarian revolutionaries, a number of Armenian patriotic committees were established in Eastern Anatolia, where the exiled Bulgarians shared revolutionary tactics and strategies with the Armenian rebels. Fighting for Armenian self-defense and spontaneous riots occurred in the cities of Erzurum, Zeitun (Süleymanlı), Van, Sason, and Muş (Sarkisian 2007: 393–394).[7] Later, many Armenian revolutionaries fighting for the freedom of their homeland found refuge in Bulgaria (Garabedyan 2001). After the Treaty of Berlin in 1878, an independent Bulgarian state was established, which had one of the most progressive constitutions of the time (Gavrilova 1999). Under the newly adopted Tarnovo Constitution, the Armenians living in the country received permanent Bulgarian citizenship, equal rights, and duties; they remained entitled to have their own municipalities, hold regular elections for local government, and make autonomous decisions (Miceva & Papazian 1998: 112). The Bulgarian Tarnovo Constitution (1879–1947) regulated in Articles 54 and 55 that all ethno-religious minorities receive guarantees of citizenship and rights equal to those of ethnic Bulgarians (Aslanian 1993: 201). Immediately after the liberation—on March 15, 1878—the Plovdiv City Council, adopting the first city plan, allocated a 12-hectare plot of land for an Armenian cemetery to be created between the Orthodox and Catholic cemetery parks. However, after being initially included in the Principality of Bulgaria according to the Treaty of San Stefano, the city of Plovdiv was

---

7   This was the period when Armenians started translating literature coming from Bulgaria, such as the rebellious novels of Lyuben Karavelov, articles by Hristo Botev, revolutionary memoirs, Zahari Stoyanov's biography of revolutionary Vasil Levski, and the novel *Pod Igoto* ("Under Yoke") by Ivan Vazov (Iliev 2001: 363).

assigned to the territory of Eastern Rumelia later that year, still under the Ottoman Empire, a situation that persisted until 1885, the year of the revolts that led to the so-called Bulgarian unification. At that time, the city counted around 33,500 inhabitants, of which 45% were Bulgarians, 25% Greeks, 21% Turks, 6% Jews, and 3% Armenians. Armenians in Plovdiv mediated contacts with Egypt and Western European countries, while bringing their capital in Bulgaria from former Armenian centers in Constantinople and other cities of the Ottoman Empire.

It is also important to mention the role of Armenian printers in the country: almost all publishing activity (newspapers and books) in this period was carried out in Armenian printing houses. After the Bulgarians achieved independence in 1878, Armenian publishers in Bulgaria cast the first printing characters in the Bulgarian alphabet (until then produced in Western Europe) and contributed to the establishment of a printing industry in the country (Garabedyan 2001b: 263). It is important to remark that Armenians in the Ottoman Empire had a long history of printing activity, dating back to the second half of the 16th century.[8]

As early as the 1880s, the Bulgarian press published articles about the most important events in the country's Armenian colony, informed Bulgarians about the customs and traditions of the Armenian inhabitants,

---

8   Indeed, the first Armenian press in Constantinople was founded by Apkar Tibir Toghatetsi, who printed the first Armenian book there in 1567, *Pokr Keraganutyun gam Aypenaran*, ("Short Grammar and Alphabet") (Köker 2012: 73). This first Armenian press was short-lived, and it wasn't until the 17th century that a whole generation of Armenian publishers and booksellers emerged in the city, with the establishment of some fifty printing houses that published in many languages, including Greek, Bulgarian, Turkish, Italian, German, Arabic, Serbian, and others. However, the real emergence of printing houses for modern publishing purposes in Constantinople took place in the 19th century: from 1832 to the mid-1860s, about fifty Armenian newspapers appeared regularly in Constantinople, including several in Turkish but with Armenian letters. In the second half of the 19th century, there were seven printing houses in Constantinople owned by Armenians. The first Bulgarian printing house was established in Constantinople, thanks to Tadey Divichiyan, (1810–1878) Armenian, publisher, printer, and bookseller, a polyglot speaking not only Armenian and Bulgarian but also Greek, Turkish, and Italian in 1844, called "Slavo-Bulgarian Typography" (Voillery 2012: 189, Ormandjyan 2001: 295).

praised their refined, ancient culture, and promoted a discourse of solidarity against the common enemy, the Turkish authorities.[9] For example, in 1881 the local newspaper *Marica* wrote: "The Armenians have never been our opponents; on the contrary, we have continually received moral support from their press and their influential media" (Erniasyan 2005: 4). The Plovdiv Newspaper wrote in 1890: "Although at various times numerous conquerors seized Armenia and destroyed it, tried to annihilate the Armenian nation, it withstood the test for more than 4,000 years, overcame suffering and persecution, survives to this day, keeps its nationality alive and today shows signs of political revival, while many neighboring, incomparably stronger nations (...) have disappeared from the face of the earth" (Erniasyan 2005: 4).

2.2. Refugees: From the Hamidian Massacres to the Genocide

For the official Armenian historiography, based on both collective and personal narratives, the turning point in recent Armenian history is the tragic persecution of Armenians in the last years of the Ottoman Empire, which began with the so-called "Hamidian massacres" in 1894–1896 (Adjemian & Nichanian 2018). In the mid-1890s, indeed the Ottoman government, led by Sultan Abdul Hamid II, openly pursued a plan to solve the "Armenian question" by exterminating its subjects. In this context, Bulgaria offered hospitality to the refugees given the long presence of the Armenian community in the country and granted certain benefits, including tax exemption for five years (Konstantinova & Načev 2019: 26). In this way, solidarity and empathy toward a Christian population perceived as victims of injustice were solidified. Between 1894 and 1896 alone, tens of thousands (estimates put the number at around 50,000, see Konstantinova & Načev 2019: 26) of Armenian refugees arrived in the country, transported by Bulgarian ships across the Black Sea. The tragic events of the Armenian refugees are also reflected in the Bulgarian local press of the time, which

---

9   The first periodical publication in the Bulgarian territories takes place in Varna during 1884 and the newspaper bears the name *Huys*, "Hope." It is published in the Armenian language but with Latin characters.

published articles about the crimes committed by the Ottoman authorities. For example, in 1896, a local newspaper wrote the following: "More than a hundred thousand Armenians have been persecuted and killed so far in Constantinople, Sivas, Diyarbakır, Trebizond, and these new horrendous crimes, even worse than the previous ones, show us what an Asiatic government is capable of, a savage Sultan" (Agukian 1995).

Many Bulgarian newspapers of that time, such as *Novo Vreme*, *Den*, *Plovdiv*, *Marica*, *Balkanska Zora*, openly expressed opinions of disdain against the Ottoman government and sympathy for the persecuted Armenians. These facts also inspired the translations of works from Armenian literature, especially the works of Rafael Patkanian, one of the most important Armenian poets, who in his works (such as the poem *The Tears of Arak*, which had a great influence on the Bulgarian audience) tried to awaken the national consciousness of the Armenian people.

Peyo Yavorov, Bulgarian writer, poet, and revolutionary, was in contact with Armenian refugees arriving in Bulgaria, and touched by their stories and circumstances. He published his poem *Armenci* ("Armenians") in the magazine *Misäl* in the early 1900s, becoming the first writer to express his sympathy with the Armenian fate in an artistic composition. *Armenci* is also the first poem in Bulgarian literature to unfold the theme of exile—the great theme of a foreigner seeking refuge in a foreign land (Georgieva 2008: 111).

The verses of *Armenci* describe the desperate grief of the refugees who were forced to leave their homeland knowing that they could never return:

> Wretched exiles, rare survivors
> Of a brave and martyr race
> Children of a captive mother
> Heroes with no resting place.
> Far from home in squalid hovels
> Sick and pale from lack of sleep.
> See them drink to drown their sorrows
> Hear them sing and, singing, weep!
> (...)
> See them scatter everywhere
> As the ruthless, bloody tyrant
> Waves his sabre in the air!
> They have left their country bleeding
> And paternal homes ablaze.

> Only taverns offer welcome
> To these wretched emigres.
> Here they sing...
> Wild songs, for savage
> Injuries erode their hearts
> Bitter thoughts their senses ravage
> Every tear is hot and smarts...

Yavorov's poem has been described as "the most profound example of brotherhood among these peoples, carved into the people's consciousness to this day" (Markov 2001: 17). This text, which is now included in all Bulgarian school anthologies, is also read by the Armenians in Armenia, who have translated it into their own language and dedicate statues and plaques to its author.[10]

On April 24, 1915, the first organized deportation of the Armenian intellectual class from what was then known as Constantinople to the city of Ankara took place. This deportation was the prelude to the annihilation of nearly the entire Armenian population (Kévorkian 2006: 251). The main strategist behind the persecution of the Armenians was the Ottoman Interior Minister Talaat Pasha, who belonged to the Young Turk movement (Deukmejian 1992: XII).

In the months and years that followed, the Armenian Genocide perpetrated by the Ottoman authorities claimed an enormous number of victims, up to 1.5 million Armenians. It also led to a further dispersal of the Armenian population that had survived the Genocide beyond the borders of present-day Turkey, leaving multiethnic Constantinople and the towns and villages in the areas of historic Armenia (Karanian 2015) in Eastern Anatolia. After the end of World War I, in the years between 1922 and 1926, hundreds of thousands of Armenian survivors abandoned the Ottoman territories, contributing to the formation of a new global diaspora.

---

10 In February 2019, on the occasion of the 120th anniversary of the composition of this poem, a delegation of Armenians from Plovdiv presided over the commemorative events in the poet's hometown of Chirpan in front of the bust of the poet.

Figure 2.1. Statue of Bulgarian Poet Peyo Yavorov at the Entrance of the Armenian Community Complex [Credits: G.S.].

After the government of Aleksandar Stamboliyski decided to open the borders of his country to them in 1923, tens of thousands of Armenians came to Bulgaria (Miceva 2001: 18). While some of them went on to France, the United States, and Canada, others stayed in Plovdiv to start a new life. The positive reception of Armenian refugees by Bulgarian authorities and the existence of a historic Armenian community in Plovdiv were crucial factors that encouraged many of these people to stay. The survivors were holders of the Nansen Passport, a special document issued in 1922 to help war refugees build a new life in the country they wanted. After their settlement, the country had about 25–35,000 Armenian inhabitants. With the influx of new refugees, Plovdiv confirmed its multiethnic urban character (Wagenstein 2002) and became fertile ground for the further development of important cultural institutions that preserve the ethnolinguistic identity of Armenians to this day. Solidarity also came from the Armenians who were already living in the city: the Tomasyan tobacco factory was made available to Armenian refugees, and each of the 15–20 rooms in this building in the center of Plovdiv housed at least a family. Stepan Hindliyan's house in Plovdiv was also turned into a shelter to dozens of Armenians. Bulgarian policy was particularly sensitive to the welfare of this community. The difficult situation in which the Christian subjects of the Ottoman Empire found themselves for more than 400 years contributed to the solidarity and compassion of Bulgarians toward the Armenian population, whom they perceived as innocent victims of an "Oriental" injustice. At the time of the Genocide, Bulgarian newspapers devoted attention to the issue: photographs and articles mentioned in a booklet published by Stepan Agukyan on the 80th anniversary of the Armenian Genocide in 1995 testify to how the Bulgarian press helped raise public awareness of the persecutions of Armenians in the collapsing Ottoman Empire (Agukian 1995).

2.3. Language Issues in the Interwar Period

In the years between the two world wars, Armenian refugees began to rebuild their lives from scratch in the new Bulgarian environment. A very interesting fact about this community is that most of them, contrary to what we may think, spoke Turkish and rarely Armenian: they came from different cities of Anatolia, but also from Eastern Thrace, such as Rodosto (Tekirdağ), Edirne, and Constantinople.

Sometimes they knew the Armenian alphabet, but they used it to write the Turkish language. Entire books and even epitaphs were written in Turkish with Armenian characters, which can be found on tombstones as well as on the inscriptions of some icons in Armenian churches (Miceva 2001: 153). When their children began to learn the Armenian language at the Armenian school, they also started studying it with them.

It could be argued that the Turkish language, despite being the mother tongue of many Armenian Genocide survivors, represents a kind of traumatic language for some of them, as it was associated with the suffering and painful extermination of most of the Armenian community in Ottoman Turkey. Genocide survivor Suren Vetsigian, who settled in Plovdiv, in his memoir *Autobiography. His Guiding Hand to Serve My People,* lamented the fact that many Armenian refugees in Greece spoke Turkish instead of Armenian, while it was unthinkable for him to communicate with other survivors in that language. The case of Suren Vetsigian was particularly tragic. As a child, during the Armenian Genocide in the late summer of 1915 in the area of his hometown of Shabin Karahisar (in what is now the Giresun Province in the Black Sea region of Northeastern Turkey), he had been forced to painfully give up his Armenian identity after losing his parents and being taken in as a servant by a Turkish man in the village of Ghayi.[11] Vetsigian was afraid to speak Armenian: "[W]e were afraid to talk to each other, for we were accused of talking Armenian" (Vetsigian 2014: 50). This form of enslavement was common among the younger Armenian survivors: at that moment, the girls and boys were converted to Islam and either Kurdified or Turkified in language and customs (Adalian 2013: 127).

As mentioned above, an Armenian press in Plovdiv had emerged in the last years of the 19th century (Hayrabedyan 1994: 105); after the arrival of the last wave of Armenian refugees in Bulgaria, the need for a stable journalistic press became even more urgent (Miceva, Papazian-Tanielian 2007: 436). The Armenian press focused its reporting on the interests of its own community. From that moment on, one of the main topics was the coverage of the Genocide and its aftermath: from the horrors experienced to the search for the missing, the reception of the refugees to the problems of their integration into Bulgarian society. Some of the Armenian newspapers published in Bulgaria in this period show us the heterogeneity of the language use of this community: there were some publications in Turkish

---

11 Being recognized as a Christian child, thus as a "giaour," posed then a serious danger, and as an Armenian, a double risk. Suren and his little brother Horen had thus to renounce their faith and have their names changed. Consequently, the Armenian language too became a taboo.

but with Armenian characters, in Armenian with Latin characters, but many of the newspapers appeared in Armenian with Armenian characters and with sections in Bulgarian and French, such as the newspaper *Marzig* ("Exercise") issued in Plovdiv. In general, it can be said that the Armenian press published in Plovdiv in the interwar period was very diverse in terms of the target audience and content. Among the Armenian newspapers of the interwar period published in Plovdiv, we can mention the *Usumnaran* ("School"), an Armenian monthly for children and youth, the Journal of the Armenian Mekhitarist School (the Armenian Catholic Congregation); the *Parossi Dzidzagh* ("The Laughter of Paros"), a humorous weekly newspaper, issued by the Armenian General Union for Physical Education, and Scouts *Homenetmen*, which dealt with social, sports, and scouting articles; the newspaper *Hayasdan* ("Armenia"), the newspaper of the Armenian national revolutionary party *Dashnaktsutyun* (Ivančev 1969: 8). A very interesting case is that of *Garmir Lourer* ("Red News"), a monthly newspaper of the Armenian section of the Bulgarian Communist Party. It is the first communist newspaper in Armenian in Europe and contains a lot of historical information about the Communist International, the Polish Communist Manifesto Party, the Baku Congress, the program of the Russian Communist Party, the Armenian political parties, the workers' movement in Turkey, the first conference of Armenian communists in Bulgaria, the national policy of Soviet Armenia, and so on (Ivančev 1969: 9). Another important publication is *Nor Ashkhar* ("New World"), an organ of the Bulgarian Communist Party, a group of the 6th Communist International. It contains articles and information about life in Soviet Armenia, the second conference of the Armenian groups of the Bulgarian Communist Party, Kemalism and the Turkish Communists, Karl Liebknecht and Rosa Luxemburg, the congress of Armenian Communists in Berlin, and criticism of the Bulgarian bourgeoisie (Ivančev 1969: 12).

2.4. Armenian Life under Bulgarian Communism

For the Armenian community of Plovdiv, one of the consequences of the establishment of the communist regime in Bulgaria after World War II was the impact on its economic activities. One of the most significant cases concerned the Tomasyan tobacco factory, which was expropriated and nationalized by the communist authorities after 1946 (Zlatkova 2023). Another unfavorable effect regarded the activities of the Mekhitarist school. This institution, founded in 1928, was the second Armenian school in the city of Plovdiv, belonging to the Mekhitarist community of Armenian Catholics. The teaching here was conducted in Armenian and French by the religious fathers, and it was a private school, which had a special character connected with their culture and spiritual program, although its curriculum was secular. This school ceased its educational activities in 1948 when the communist authorities ordered its closure because of its religious orientation. In this context, the school's valuable library was also destroyed. It contained more than 1,000 old books of great value, which the students knew well since the Mekhitarist fathers made them read in order to practice their Armenian for at least one hour every Sunday (Ozanyan 2003: 23).

In the immediate postwar period, a so-called "repatriation movement" (Laycock 2012, Konstantinova & Načev 2019: 25ff) emerged, in which almost 100,000 Armenians from the worldwide diaspora answered the call to return to their "homeland" as part of a Soviet resettlement plan. In total, 3% of them were constituted by Bulgarian Armenians (Panossian 1998: 186). However, this "homeland" was in Soviet Armenia and not in the historic Armenian territories in Turkey, and thus represented only a "substitute" homeland. Many Armenians from Bulgaria and Plovdiv joined, partly because of the terrible economic crisis and partly for patriotic reasons or a personal sense of belonging, and as a consequence, the number of students enrolled in the Armenian school, once close to 800, dropped to only 400. Plovdiv writer and scholar Suren Vetsigian wrote in 1947 on this issue:

> Now under the terrible economic conditions we are very anxious for a way out. Many Armenians find it by going to Soviet Armenia. Since our aim is not a mere physical existence, but a useful existence for the cause of Christ, emigration to Armenia is for us suicidal. (Vetsigian 2014: 131)

Furthermore, although it was not easy to leave Bulgaria during the Communist period, about five thousand Armenians managed to emigrate to the United States, in the 1960s (Berberyan 2019: 11). In the years between 1946 and 1965, the number of Armenians in Bulgaria was around

21,600–21,900 people, and the biggest population lived in Plovdiv, with around 8,000 members of this community (Konstantinova & Načev 2019: 36).

As a result of the anti-religious policies, the activities of the Armenian churches were severely curtailed in this period. All Armenian organizations were dissolved,[12] newspapers and magazines were closed, and the cultural and educational organization of Armenians in Bulgaria *Erevan* was founded together with a newspaper of the same name (Papazian-Tanielian 2016: 195). The latter was the only Armenian newspaper active during communism, and like all printed publications in the Bulgarian territory during that period, it was also a propaganda tool of the government. At the same time, however, it represented the only opportunity to express Armenian self-awareness. The weekly[13] *Erevan* was written only in Armenian (until 1981, when it became bilingual, with content in both Bulgarian and Armenian), in the Eastern variant of this language, and despite state control, the newspaper strove to inform about the cultural and social life of the community and the development of Soviet Armenia. Its aim was also to reflect the life of Armenians in the Diaspora, and to keep Armenian consciousness alive in its readers, preserving the love for the Armenian homeland and for the rich culture of the past in the "lost lands" (Panossian 1998: 184) of Western Armenia. Nevertheless, agitations and protests in the local community of Plovdiv took place against the editorial line taken by the newspaper and against the orientation of the activities promoted by the *Erevan* organization (Interview to Mr. Sahak Tchalykian, editor of the weekly *Vahan*, in October 2010). Over the years, the success of the weekly began to pose a threat in the eyes of the party power in Bulgaria, due to the illegitimate Armenian patriotism and the excessive influence of the Armenian world outside the country. The newspaper therefore had to adapt to the party's guidelines and limit itself to reporting only on events that affected the Bulgarian-Armenian community.

---

12 Two exceptions in this city were the Aram Khachaturian Choir and the Erebuni Vocal and Instrumental Ensemble.

13 Although it had started as a biweekly.

One of the most significant linguistic consequences for the fate of the Armenian community in Plovdiv during this period was the introduction of the teaching of the Eastern variant of the Armenian language in place of the Western one, in accordance with Soviet Union directives. The central leadership of the Erevan organization adopted this decision in 1946, which did not meet the wishes of the Armenian community in Bulgaria, since its members spoke, wrote, and read the Western variant of the language that also differed grammatically from the Eastern one. The teaching of the Eastern Armenian language was established along with the "Abeghyan" Soviet orthography, which, with the reform of 1922, had introduced some changes in the use of certain letters of the alphabet according to a phonologically "simplifying" logic. Armenians in Bulgaria were not feeling comfortable with this new variant, and the use of the written form of the Armenian language in everyday life was greatly affected.

> This decision had no real pedagogical argument, but was the result of a purely political choice due to the pro-Soviet orientation. We pupils were taught Eastern Armenian with the help of textbooks that the school received free of charge from Soviet Armenia, but could not speak it properly at school, let alone use it as a written and oral language in daily life. (Interview with Tutunjyan School Director Viržinija Garabedyan, February 2010)

The practice of speaking Armenian at home remained intact until the event that most negatively impacted the history of the Armenian community in Plovdiv. In 1976, the Communist Central Committee made a choice of enormous significance, opting for the closure of the last minority school with mother language instruction still active in the country, namely the Tutunjyan Armenian School in Plovdiv. Armenians rebelled and tried to resist, but any protest was immediately suppressed through arrests and threats. This traumatic event had an immediate impact not only on the schooling of Armenian children but also on the use of the Armenian language: children began to stop using it; they gradually lost it on an active and even passive level. Of little help were the informal classes of Armenian language at the so-called Saturday school organized by the AGBU/Parekordzagan volunteer group to remedy the serious problem (Miceva 2001: 141–142).

Gradually, as the new generations had to complete their education in Bulgarian schools, the loss of the mother tongue in the classroom was accompanied by the breaking of the tradition of speaking Armenian in the families. As school director Garabedyan relates:

> The cultural damage to the Armenian community, as to any other minority in the same situation, was enormous. The language pattern of the population has changed considerably as a result, and it is a fact today that in most Armenian families it is no longer clear which language is spoken most often... So there was such a disruption that there were discontinuities in the level of knowledge of the Armenian language, and this then clearly affected the following generations, up to the present day. (Interview with Tutunjyan School Director Viržinija Garabedyan, February 2010)

2.5. The Post-Socialist Transition's Impact on Armenians

The democratic changes of November 10, 1989 were a turning point for Bulgarian society and also had very positive effects on the Armenian community. The Armenian school was reopened, as well as the AGBU/ Parekordzagan Organization, the scout organization, and the Armenian Red Cross organization. This date allowed continuity, albeit with an interruption, in the cultural traditions of Armenians in Bulgaria. Linguistically, the main problem in this early period was that generations had grown up without the possibility to learn their alphabet and were thus unable to read the Armenian language. Moreover, in many families the lack of written knowledge was accompanied by a diminished interest in the history and culture of their people (Miceva 2001: 144). In the new post-communist era, therefore, an urgent need was felt to solve this problem, by reactivating the values of the Armenian identity and fostering feelings of belonging to a distinct ethnocultural community. Many of the Armenians who did not know the Armenian alphabet were already at an age when they became aware of the value systems associated with their Armenian affiliation. They felt the desire to use the language and script of their ancestors, but none of those who were already parents could help their children to take the first steps toward education in the Armenian language. The need, therefore, arose to set up temporary language courses for young people and adults, a situation that, according to some of my older informants, was somewhat reminiscent of the time when newcomers from Armenia mainly used the Turkish language and learned Armenian together with their children, who were pupils at the Armenian school in Plovdiv.

It was also at this time that two new newspapers were finally established in Bulgaria: *Hayer* ("Armenians") in Burgas, in Bulgarian only, and *Vahan* ("Shield") in Plovdiv, bilingual. The *Erevan* newspaper continued to be printed, and in 2004, the monthly (later biweekly) *Parekordzagani Tzain* in Plovdiv also saw the light of day. The *Vahan* newspaper also cooperated with the Erevan Cultural Association for some period (in the early 2000s) in the issuing of an annual magazine called *Nie-Menk* ("We" in Bulgarian and Armenian, respectively), which collected articles on the most important topics in Bulgarian-Armenian history, including traditions and holidays, written tradition, education, etc. When dealing with the subject of the periodical press, one cannot avoid mentioning politics, that is, the fact that the *Vahan* newspaper is more associated with the *Dashnaktsutyun*[14] (Armenian Revolutionary Federation, with a socialist orientation), while the *Parekordzagani Tzain* is associated with the *Ramgavar* Party (Armenian Democratic Liberal Party). This is important to understand the extent to which the "symbolic cultivation" of collective identity carried out by certain institutions within the diasporic community, based on a discourse involving myths and emotions, collides with the reality of the split between two factions that tend to live parallel lives and, in many cases, ignore each other. This division sometimes leads to a kind of internal struggle within the community for certain positions of power, especially the important position of leadership of the Armenian school. The weekly newspaper *Parekordzagani Tzain*, which is detailed further in Chapter 5, deals much less with current political issues and focuses more on reporting on events in the Armenian community in Plovdiv and in Bulgaria and on disseminating the numerous activities of the AGBU. The newspaper *Vahan* published weekly used to be bilingual, with about 25% of articles in Armenian and the rest in Bulgarian, but in recent years the proportion of Armenian articles has been further reduced.[15] In this periodical publication, articles dealing with the topic of the Armenian Genocide are accompanied by denunciations of the failure of Turkey in the first place, but

---

14 *Tashnagtsutyun* in Western Armenian.
15 In addition, the bilingual Armenian weekly Erevan, published in Sofia, is also read by members of the Armenian diaspora in Plovdiv.

also of most countries in the world, to acknowledge in an official way the tragedy experienced by the Armenian people over a century ago. As mentioned, the *Vahan* has a political line that is related to the activities of the *Dashnaktsutyun* Party, and this is reflected in the way the identity rhetoric is conducted: it is much more focused on the contemporaneity of the Republic of Armenia and on the even stronger political symbols of the Nagorno-Karabakh war, its heroes and its enemies. Constant reference is made to the geopolitical situation in the Caucasus and the interests of the Turks, who are allied with the Azeris, in further isolating Armenia, which is severely burdened by the closure of the borders with the two countries and the resulting economic difficulties in trade.

This attention to current political and geopolitical issues meets the needs of a certain segment of the local Armenian population, especially members of the younger diaspora, that is, the diaspora from the Republic of Armenia that emerged after the collapse of the Soviet Union. Since the 1990s, many Armenians have started arriving in Bulgaria to join their relatives who had previously settled and to seek better job opportunities, a phenomenon that continues today. The distinction between the two main groups within the Armenian community, that is the recent post-1991 diaspora and the diaspora dating back to the arrival of refugees in 1922 or earlier, was not immediately evident to me, and it was only over time that I noticed how distinct the boundary between them is.

Plovdiv is home to about 2,000 Armenians out of a total population of around 5,300 Armenians in the country, according to official Bulgarian figures (Bulgarian Census 2021). However, according to unofficial Armenian figures, there are about 4,000 in Plovdiv and 20,000[16] in the whole country.[17] They are well integrated into Bulgarian society, and its members often occupy a prominent socioeconomic position in the city (Papazian-Tanielian 2016: 194). In today's situation in Plovdiv, Armenians

---

16 See, for example, the recent article: https://arminfo.info/full_news.php?id= 68027&lang=3.
    Sometimes, Armenians in Plovdiv refer to even higher figures.
17 According to internal estimates by Armenian organizations, there are up to 50,000 Armenians in Bulgaria, including about 35,000 'new' Armenians who have migrated from the post-Soviet Republic of Armenia (Hovyan 2011).

are confronted on a daily basis not only with the Bulgarian majority but also with Turks, Romas, Pomaks, Jews, Greeks, Russians, Ukrainians, and others. In the context of the title of the European Capital of Culture held by Plovdiv in 2019, many initiatives have taken place to promote the ethnolinguistic, cultural, and religious diversity of the communities in the city (Bid Book 2019). This theme was developed through a series of activities aimed at presenting the complex and diverse mosaic of Plovdiv to both residents and external visitors. During the year of the European Capital of Culture in Plovdiv, special recognition was given to Armenian culture in the city and its surroundings. For example, events dedicated to Armenian culture and cuisine provided an opportunity to learn more about the most emblematic Armenian traditions. The occasion also served to strengthen the relations between Bulgaria and the Republic of Armenia: in this regard, an initiative was supported in the capital Yerevan, consisting of a photo exhibition about the Armenian diaspora in Plovdiv, its traditions and cultural and historical sites in the Old Town, realized by a local photographer. The favorable European context of support has given new impetus and encouragement to the legitimization of visible difference in ethnocultural terms, which has led to the creation of intercultural initiatives, including the culinary art fair "Ethno Kitchen on Wheels," the celebration of the International Day for Ethnic Tolerance[18] (November 16), and others. Relations between Armenians and Bulgarians continue to be characterized by a positive and cooperative attitude: the interest of Bulgarians in Armenian culture has increased in recent years, a fact that has stimulated the publication of numerous works on Armenian history and literature, thanks also to the Chair of Armenian Studies established at the Kliment Ohridski University of Sofia.

---

[18] Officially declared by the United Nations as "International Day of Tolerance," in Bulgaria it is called "ethnic tolerance."

3. Language as an Idealized Space of Belonging

Abstract: This chapter focuses on the symbolic function played by language in the Armenian diaspora, examining its value as a marker of cultural distinctiveness and as an element that supports collective cohesion and remembrance practices. Patterns of language use from the perspective of transnational belonging are examined, with attention to the relationship between the Western and Eastern variants of the language. The relevance of the autochthonous Armenian writing system is also here discussed in this chapter.

Keywords: symbolic value of language, Mesrop Mashtots's alphabet, language and identity, Western and Eastern Armenian, Armenian literacy

3.1. Language, Myth, and Symbolic Imaginary in the Diaspora

The language context is a crucial element for analyzing the role of symbols in promoting internal cohesion. For this community in the Plovdiv diaspora, as elsewhere in the world, the Armenian language plays indeed a predominantly "symbolic" role and does not reach high levels of practical utility. In light of this, the retention of the language is presented by local elites more as an emotional connection to an ethnic past than as an effective means of communication. As far as the symbolic role of the language is concerned, the graphic form, namely the unique Armenian alphabet, is particularly suitable for acting as an effective boundary marker. As Barth (1998 [1969]) noted, in the context of social construction of cultural difference among different ethnic groups, it is not the cultural content but rather the symbolic boundary markers such as language, religion, and folklore that contribute to preserving the identity of a given community and require anthropological study (Barth 1998: 15). In this respect, it is important to remark that, over the course of their history, Armenians have been in constant contact with other communities throughout their history and have drawn from these encounters a reason to assert their identity even more strongly.

The focus on the mother tongue and its spiritualization is widespread among Armenians who have been separated from their native territories (Aghanian 2007: 172): "[h]aving served as the major instrument of national survival across the centuries, language has become the object of a cult, has been sanctified by the Church and has virtually symbolized the national identity" (Oshagan 1986: 224). Language in itself is of great importance, as many believe that it is not possible to be Armenian without speaking, writing, and reading it: it determines who you are and who you are not; it is a way to define the boundaries of a group. This gives rise to specific visions of Armenian identity that can be defined as "essentialists" and "traditionalists," advocating the idea that speaking the Armenian language and being immersed in the Armenian "ethnic" culture are fundamental prerequisites for "being Armenian" (Tchilingirian 2018). Language is a useful tool to create imagined communities (Anderson 1991): in the absence of a territory, it serves as a space for imagining the nation while connecting the current generation with those who preceded it. In order for a language to be passed on from one generation to the next, it must have symbolic meaning (Drost-Abgarian 1997): children must receive positive reinforcement through what Fishman, the founder of the field of the sociology of language, calls the "home-family-neighborhood-community" arena (Fishman 1991: 466).

Sometimes retaining the language is just a matter of learning a few keywords or phrases to use in the family: greetings, words concerning food, songs, hymns, or poems—all of which fall squarely within the realm of the symbolic.

When we reflect on the use of writing in Western societies, we find that it focuses almost exclusively on the communicative function, that is, on the transmission of information; however, this is not always the case, since in other societies we encounter forms of writing that may acquire different forms of signification, as a means of cultural expression (Cardona 1982: 6). This is the case for the Armenians, for whom writing conveys messages of a highly symbolic nature. Furthermore, in situations that involve relatively small social groups, as is, for example, the case of diaspora and minority contexts, the field of writing is intended to be open to all, and there would be no reason to make it esoteric, given the general usefulness of the signs it ciphers. The domain of writing and reading in Armenian has always remained a priority value in the ethnocultural ideology that guides the forces promoting a distinct Armenian identity. However, since its practice cannot be carried far enough, more direct and appropriate ways are taken to develop positive ideas regarding the alphabet that produce another level of signification in which the subject of writing is embedded.

Culture and cultural diversity are quite complex concepts that are open to a wide range of interpretations: as far as cultural values are concerned, every ethnic group has a set of values considered fundamental to its vitality and integrity that form the pillars on which the entire collective identification system is built. This hierarchy of values may vary widely among ethnic groups, so that some give priority to language, others to religion, others perhaps to family structure, etc. In the case of the Armenians in Plovdiv, the written language is certainly at the top of this value system, as can be deduced, for example, from the following sentences in the magazine *Menk*, published by the Armenian newspaper *Vahan* in cooperation with the Erevan Association:

> This is the right place to talk about the colossal importance and role of Mashtots's invention of the alphabet in the preservation of our nation. Thanks to it, not only has Armenian culture survived, but also an immense literature has been created in our mother tongue, which to this day holds an honorable place in the history of written culture and in the cultural heritage of the world. Even more important is the political significance of the appearance of Mashtots's letters: they tirelessly raise Armenian consciousness and become the best shield against the assimilation policy of foreign conquerors. The entire 1,600-year history of Armenia up to the present day proves this. (Topakbashyan 2003: 41)

The issue of writing practices in the case of Armenians is thus strongly related to the role of the alphabet created by Mesrop Mashtots in sustaining discourses on ethnic identity and collective memory.

3.2. A Brief History of the Armenian Alphabet

In their historical territory between Asia Minor, Mesopotamia, and the Caucasus, the Armenians were confronted with peoples who had long been literate: cuneiform writing was already widespread in the second millennium B.C., and in its local variants served as a means of representation for many languages: from Hittite to Elamite, from Urartian to Old Persian. After contact with the Urartian civilization, the Armenians adopted some of its elements, including linguistic ones, but not the cuneiform script, whose use, moreover, soon declined under the pressure of more flexible and functional alphabets. Aramaic, the official language of Achaemenid Persia in its relations with neighboring peoples, and Greek, which had been in circulation since Hellenism, were also represented by their own scripts: Armenians made use of the languages spoken in the region and for a long time did not consider it necessary to record the national language in an own writing system (Uluhogian 1986: 117). However, when the Sassanids ascended the Persian throne in the first half of the 2nd century A.D. and instituted a policy of restoring the old centralist ideals of the Achaemenids, the threat of assimilation began to become more real for the Armenians. The official conversion to Christianity in the early 4th century and the pressure of Mazdaic proselytizing by Sassanid Persia were distinct but simultaneous factors that contributed to the stronger formation of an Armenian national identity. An additional factor was the division of the highly multicultural Armenian territories into two zones of influence, Roman and Persian, around 387, a fact that placed them at the crossroads of great civilizations and exposed them to multiple assimilation threats (Grosby 2005: 23). At this delicate moment in history, at the beginning of the 5th century (405), the creation of a unique alphabet for the translation of the Holy Scriptures into Armenian occurred as a culturally outstanding and politically momentous event which greatly contributed in the survival of this language and in ensuring its continuity over the centuries. Mesrop Mashtots' "paternity" of the Armenian alphabet has been acknowledged by both Western and Armenian scholars, who argue that the will of proselytizing the Armenians by translating the Bible was a crucial factor in creating one of the most important aspects of Armenian identity (Maksoudian 2006: 157). In place of the various influences and traditions that separated the Armenian people and the Church,[19] language, faith, and script were thus able to merge into a national experience expressed in the

---

19 "From the very beginning, the Armenian Church had a legal and circumscriptional configuration on an ethnic basis, so that it had at its head a bishop responsible for the entire territory of the Kingdom" Zekiyan 2000: 199 (my translation).

local language that was useful for the advancement of Christian Armenia and its religious and cultural aspirations (Zekiyan 2000: 199).

In addition, many modern Armenian scholars have attributed secular, political, and socioeconomic reasons to the invention of this alphabet and the successive development of literacy. This corresponded mainly to the Soviet line of interpretation, according to which the creation of Armenian letters had become an unpostponable necessity: these were essential to the establishment of schools and the creation of written literature, as well as to ensure the development and victory of the emerging religious and feudal ideology (Maksoudian 2006: 2).

Without any doubt, the Armenian alphabet was created by Mesrop Mashtots through the convergence of all these factors in the period after the conversion to Christianity in 301 (Ferrari 2016b: 13) when local political authorities understood the importance of distinguishing themselves from their neighbors to avoid assimilation and started creating and affirming a specific consciousness of "being Armenian." Mashtots could not have embarked on such a mission to spread literacy without the support of the country's leaders at the time—the head of the temporal power, King Vramshapuh, and the spiritual power, the Catholicos Sahak, who were personally involved in the creation of the Armenian script: the cultural enlightenment movement was supported by the ecclesiastical hierarchy, the royal court, and the nobility.[20]

The literacy movement of the 5th century in Armenia affected the spiritual and social life of the Armenian people, as well as the political sphere. The translation of sacred texts into Armenian contributed to the development of liturgy and rituals, and the liturgical language gave Christianity, which was flourishing in Armenia, its own local identity. The development of the Armenian tradition persisted until the first decades of the 8th century when the process was interrupted by a series of revolts against the Arab caliphate, which proved disastrous for Armenian culture, church, and nobility. After the end of the Kingdom of Cilicia in 1375, Armenians

---

20 In particular, King Vramashapuh sent young men to them to learn the alphabet and arranged for the establishment of schools throughout his kingdom, himself providing the funding for these.

no longer had a state of their own and remained subject to various foreign rulers (Walker 2005: 4–11); nevertheless, they retained a sense of their own cultural identity through their own church, their own language, and, of course, their own script.

The alphabet created by Mesrop Mashtots in the early 5th century is still used today with only a few minor changes. The original alphabet consisted of 36 letters, one character for each phoneme in Classical Armenian as spoken in the central regions of historical Armenia. Therefore, the question of a new orthography to represent the phonemes of a language played a crucial role at that time, when the other alphabets—Syriac, Greek, Aramaic—proved to be not suitable at all. The success of Mashtots's enterprise also depended on his decision to create an alphabetic system whose basic principle was to represent a single sound of the oral language with a single letter. This is a phonematic principle, and the Armenian alphabet is one of the most perfect from this point of view. As great French linguist Antoine Meillet wrote: "[O]nly after the creation of the Armenian alphabet, the translation of the Bible into Armenian and the establishment of an Armenian literature, a real Armenian culture was formed. Only from that moment the Armenian nation became truly aware of itself. And from then on it was this written language, this literature, which sustained the national feeling" (Bolognesi 2000: 8–9, my translation).

In the 12th and 13th centuries, two more letters, the long O (corresponding to Greek Ω) and Ֆ (corresponding to Greek Φ), were borrowed from Greek and placed at the end of the alphabet and became the thirty-seventh and thirty-eighth letters of the alphabet, a necessary measure due to the words borrowed from both Western and Eastern languages.

3.3. The Western and Eastern Variants of the Armenian Language

When tracing the development of the Armenian language, it is necessary to keep in mind its historical division into two variants, which took place in the mid-18th century between the Western and Eastern variants, corresponding to the dialects spoken in the cities of Constantinople and Tbilisi. These were two crucial poles of Armenian cultural and intellectual life, but subject to two different empires: the Ottoman and the Russian, respectively. The introduction of new literary forms and styles, as well as numerous new European ideas that reached Armenians in both regions, led to an increasing need to elevate the vernacular language, called *ashkharhabar*, to a modern literary language, as opposed to *grabar*, the classical liturgical language (Donabedian-Demopoulos 2018). There were of course many other dialects spoken in the traditional Armenian regions, but these two were the two main variants that emerged. Both Constantinople and Tbilisi vigorously promoted the *ashkharhabar*, and this was accomplished through the proliferation of newspapers in both variants and the development of a network of schools where modern Armenian was taught, dramatically increasing the literacy rate in the local Armenian populations. The emergence of literary works written entirely in the modern language thus legitimized its existence in both cities and their areas of influence. Today, apart from some morphological, phonological, and grammatical differences, the largely common vocabulary and rules of grammar enable users of one variant to understand the other without too much difficulty. The Republic of Armenia does not legally distinguish between the two forms and declares "Armenian" to be the official language, although de facto Eastern Armenian is the official language, as this form is used almost exclusively in all spheres of life in the country (including government, education, and media).

The Armenian language historically spoken in Plovdiv is the Western variant, the same form spoken by the Armenian diaspora in other parts of Europe, North and South America, and in most Middle Eastern countries except Iran. Due to the recent arrival of migrants from the independent Republic of Armenia, the Eastern variant is also present. Phonological differences pose the greatest challenge to the mutual intelligibility of the two variants. In the Western variant, some consonants are read as voiced, but are read as unvoiced in the other variant: for example, the letter "p" is pronounced as /b/ in Eastern Armenian, but as /p/ in the Western dialect. The Western branch of the Armenian language is a non-territorial minority language. Since it does not have the status of a state language in any country of the world, it is not a language of administration, function, and public life (Dermerguerian 1997: 22). Moreover, it enjoys no real official state protection in any country, and it is thus considered an endangered language in the diaspora worldwide (AGBU 2015). Much of the Armenian diaspora in Europe consists of descendants of refugees and exiles who survived the Genocide; thus, the Western variant is today almost exclusively a diasporic, exilic language (Chahinian & Bakalian 2016: 47).

In 2009, UNESCO classified the Western Armenian variant spoken in Turkey as a "definitely endangered" language.[21] The same consideration applies to the situation of this language in Bulgaria (interview with Ahavni Kevorkyan, March 2022). Ethnologue (2018) provides figures referring to 5,620 speakers of this language in the country. The same source also classifies Armenian in Bulgaria as an "immigrant language," a somewhat problematic claim, since Armenian has been spoken for around 1,500 years on Southeast European territories. In the diaspora, the Western branch of the Armenian language is losing speakers at a high rate, and the challenge is to ensure an appropriate institutional role for this language in the long term: this could be achieved with the support of both Bulgarian and European institutions, with the aim of enhancing the heritage of the linguistic diversity of diasporic and migrant communities on the Old Continent.

The main operating spaces of this variant are the family sphere, the school domain, and the press domain. The school area may vary according to the organization of the system of each community, but it is definitely the most important one for the transmission of the written language and national cultural values. The intellectual sphere (composed of teachers, journalists, writers, clergy, artists) represents the main functioning domain of the literary language, regarded as the engine of cultural creation and the support of thought in this variant. Finally, associative life provides another significant space for the functioning of the language.

In the Armenian linguistic landscape of Plovdiv, Western Armenian dominates the examples of public writing almost unchallenged. During my observations of the Armenian spaces of Plovdiv, I have come across only a few examples of public writing in the Eastern variety of the language: one inside the Armenian restaurant Erevan, and the other outside the Armenian Church ("I remember and I hold on"). Nevertheless, in this sense it would be inappropriate to consider the Armenian alphabet in its

---

21 www.bianet.org/english/minorities/112728-unesco-15-languages-endangered-in-turkey

difference in rendering partially different sounds in the two variants: the alphabet is visually always the same, it is what unites Armenians despite the differences, it is more than a graphic system on a phonetic basis, it becomes rather a symbolic system on which memories, values, and world views are implanted. Its use reflects the ideological component of the communities and transmits cultural knowledge. As already discussed, language itself can become one of the most value-relevant elements for a group of people and serve to create a barrier: this certainly happens in the case of Armenians vis-à-vis other peoples. In the case of the division between Western and Eastern Armenians, the issue is complex, but it cannot be said that the written language becomes a reason for difference: pride and love for one's alphabet are feelings shared by all Armenians, whether in the diaspora or not.

3.4. The Religious and Secular Cult of Mesrop Mashtots

When analyzing the patterns of Armenian life in the Diaspora, the position of the Armenian Apostolic Church cannot be overlooked: the majority of Armenians, including atheists, still see in it a symbol of integrity and national identity.[22] The other crucial historical event preceding the invention of the alphabet, the first fundamental step to "being Armenian," as mentioned, was indeed the official adoption of Christianity as early as 301. This historical fact made Armenia the first nation in the world that acknowledged Christianity as a state religion. Obviously, this helped to create a strong motivation for the adoption of an own script. It follows that the discourse on the role of religion for Armenian communities is also, to some extent, permeated by the so-called myth of ethnic election (Smith 1999). The pride for being the first nation in the world to adopt Christianity has nurtured and consolidated the belief in being a chosen people and having a divine mission to such an extent that Christianity has

---

22 The Armenian Church was already independent of the Greco-Roman Church in the 5th century, when it rejected the definition used at the Council of Chalcedon (Walker 2005: 2) on the relationship between the human and divine natures of Christ and referred to the earlier Christological definition of the Council of Ephesus (431): "one nature of God, the Word incarnate".

been genetically essentialized, according to the formula: Armenian identity = Christianity. We can certainly maintain that this sense of closeness to God and the resulting moral implications for the community also constituted a social and psychological motive for the survival of the Armenians (Aghanian 2007: 29).

Although Mashtots is the creator of the alphabet, God is the original source of the gift, and therefore the alphabet is considered "God's gift." For Armenians, thus, the connection between the alphabet and religion is indissoluble, as demonstrated by one article reporting the words pronounced by the Catholicos, the patriarch of all Armenians (the most important spiritual figure), regarding the Armenian alphabet:

> These letters are 36 soldiers who always lead us to victory. Saint Mesrop has given us the ability to speak to the Lord through these letters, and through this language we Armenians have preserved our identity as a people and have managed to form ourselves as a nation. (Viviano 2004: 3)

On this occasion, the Catholicos also emphasized the role played by this writing system in educating the people in the written language and thus in the Christian religion, a fact which allowed for the establishment of the connection between written culture and Christianity, book and Church. The churches also served as schools and as, a repository for manuscripts. Thus, they played a fundamental role not only on the spiritual but also on the ethnocultural level, since all social and cultural activities took place within its walls: they constituted the center of the community. Today, church institutions preserve the relation with the Holy See of Ejmiatsin (in the Republic of Armenia) and interacting with other organizations in the diasporas through their social and charitable organizations, and a network of newspapers and magazines. As far as language use is concerned, in the Armenian Church "Surp Kevork" in Plovdiv, although the liturgy is traditionally conducted in *grabar*, the sermons are delivered in modern language (Dermerguerian 1997: 24).

An interesting example of the practices connecting the Church with the cult of the Armenian script is the Feast of the Translator. Although Evgeniya Miceva, an eminent expert on Bulgarian Armenians, claimed that "[t]he Feast of the Translator has lost its significance today (...) and has no possibility of preservation or development. Only in the church people try to keep it alive." (Miceva 2001: 104). I believe that this anniversary, which is

Figure 3.1. Entrance to the Armenian Church "Surp Kevork" [Credits: G.S.].

celebrated every year on the second Saturday of October as "Translator's Day" (sometimes also referred to as "Day of the Translators" in the plural), is still quite alive and acquires a special significance in the ideological discourse on writing. Indeed, the Armenian community in Plovdiv gives it prominence through articles published on its media and celebrations at the Armenian school, as this day falls at the beginning of the school year. The "Translator" in question is, of course, none other than Mesrop Mashtots, but in addition to him, Catholicos Sahak is also remembered, who supported him in his work, as well as the students who were taught by them and ensured the continuation of the fundamental work.

The 5th century is portrayed in the local media as the golden century of Armenian culture, when schools flourished and the importance of writing and books was enshrined as a means of approaching the Word of God, but above all as a means of being truly Armenian. It is considered the first real "triumph of culture," and today's celebrations are intended to remind Armenians that they owe their existence primarily to the work of the translators Mesrop Mashtots and Catholicos Sahak, who succeeded in spreading the divine Word for the first time.

> Mesrop Mashtots, as a young man, has a revelation in a dream and feels called to dedicate himself to the Christian preaching. Having invented the Armenian script, he can finally devote himself to the work of translation: immediately, blessed books from Greek, Syriac and Hebrew are translated, as well as other works of ancient authors. (Erniasyan 2010: 2)

Thus, the second Saturday of October is a holiday for all Armenians, glorifying the culture that has spread to all corners of the world, including Plovdiv. The biweekly magazine *Parekordzagani Tzain* usually publishes articles on the Feast of Translators in September, explaining how the Armenian Apostolic Church celebrates such a day every October, dedicated to the creator of the Armenian alphabet and the translators of the Bible. It highlights that such a religious holiday is not limited to its canonical addressing but has a general cultural and civilizational significance. Such rhetoric is also found in the pages of the weekly *Vahan*, where it is explained that this holiday is dedicated to the event that, above all, produced Armenian culture (Vahan 2010). According to this view, the alphabet embodies the most authentic spirit of the nation, which was able to produce an entire literary tradition: its letters therefore symbolize, more than anything else, the value and level that the Armenian people have achieved. The century after the invention of the Armenian script was a century of tribulation and conquest, which, however, the Armenian people withstood by resisting the light of its translations: it comes as no surprise, thus, that the Translators were also sanctified. In Armenian culture, a specific "culture of translation" has thus existed since historical times: the Bible and the other significant works translated from Greek and Syriac were crucial elements that provided Armenians with a perspective on the importance of the past for the present and for the future. This specific historical consciousness was probably one of the factors which contributed in keeping religious and ethnic identity alive throughout the centuries, reminding Armenians that their homeland is full of sacred sites linked to their Christian past (Sarkisian 2007: 193). Thus, by honoring the Translator through various forms of celebration (in the media, in the school, in the church), the Plovdiv diaspora automatically refers to the historical time when the entire concept of the Armenian nation was forged, asserting its distinctiveness through the meaningful and symbolic tool of writing, which was already an extremely effective instrument of power.

Interestingly, Armenia is not the only country in the world where a celebration is held in honor of the translator and inventor of the national alphabet: there is another, and curiously enough, it is Bulgaria! In this country, there is a strong devotion to Saints Cyril and Methodius, the two brothers who invented the Glagolitic alphabet in the 9th century, from which the Bulgarian Cyrillic alphabet is derived. The "Day of the Holy Brothers Cyril and Methodius, of the Bulgarian alphabet, education and culture and of the Slavonic literature" falls every year on May 24 (Selvelli 2023b). In the Armenian literature of Bulgaria reference is made to the strange historical coincidence between the events in these two countries following the invention of the new writing system (Mikaelian 2010). In both cases, it was two personalities who promoted the process of literacy acquisition of the population: the brothers Cyril and Methodius for the Bulgarians, Mesrop Mashtots and Catholikos Vahak for the Armenians (Stamatov 2001: 21). Both alphabetic traditions, Bulgarian and Armenian, thus represent the rare case of an alphabetic invention that refers to historically identified signs and was sanctioned by divine inspiration, confirming its providential origin. The local Armenian writer Mikaelian, a great advocate of the cultural affinity between the Armenian and Bulgarian peoples, expressed his being intrigued by this unique similarity: "[S]o there is a natural kinship between Armenians and Bulgarians, as there was between Paulicians and Bogomils. But the most important thing is that the alphabet is original, both for Armenians and Bulgarians" (Personal interview with Hovannes Mikaelian, November 2010).

A similar juxtaposition between Bulgarians and Armenians regarding the creation of their alphabet was noticed by Giorgio Raimondo Cardona. The scholar states that in traditions where writing can be attributed to a specific creator, the invention of the alphabet is usually sanctioned by the seal of a divine appearance, which establishes its direct supernatural derivation. To Cyril, also called Constantine the Philosopher, to whom the invention of the Cyrillic script is associated, God appeared απροσδόκητος, "unexpected", in the course of the usual prayer (Cardona 1986: 59):

> As was his habit (...) the Philosopher began to pray (...) and suddenly God appeared to him (...), and immediately Constantine started to write the Gospel (...) Exemplary causal chain according to which the One who revealed the Word can also reveal to men the way to communicate it: the same Providence weaves the threads of the possibilities of communicating the Word, hands down the gift of tongues on the gathered apostles and forms the signs so that they too can speak to men. (My translation)

Also, Saint Mesrop Mashtots found the alphabet through divine revelation: according to his biographer Koriwn, Mashtots turned earnestly to God, addressing him with prayers mixed with tears, asking him day and night to reveal to him the letters he so longed for, until he suddenly saw them. Mesrop had "not a dream while sleeping, not a vision while awake, but in the depths of his heart there appeared before the eyes of his soul a right hand writing on the rock; thus the stone held the forms of the letters, like traces engraved in the snow" (Cardona 1986: 60, my translation).

The figure of Mesrop Mashtots, together with his life and death, interestingly, constitutes a topic in the newspapers and other publications of the Armenians of Plovdiv: Mashtots's story is closely connected with his greatest product, the alphabet, and therefore still attracts great attention and gratitude. The Armenian cultural milieu is imbued with a theological spirit and a reverence for the written word, as is the case in Slavic ecclesiastical culture, especially the Bulgarian one (Cardona 2009: 160): Armenians have found a second homeland in Bulgaria, where certain cultural and symbolic dynamics of identity associated with the alphabet find fertile ground and legitimization. In Armenian culture, the book is given great attention and is, in a sense, cultically revered, a fact that is fully reflected in the context of the Plovdiv diaspora, where the printing of Armenian books began in Bulgaria (Kasabian & Giligian 2008).[23] This also results in a special esthetic interpretation of the Armenian alphabet (Drücker 1995), which contributes in an imaginative way to its being perceived as more than a code of phonetic signs, also out of a sense for art (Cardona 2009: 170).

In the Armenian Church Surp Kevork, several old printed books with spiritual and secular content in the Armenian language are preserved, which were printed in different cities of the world where Armenians used to live, such as Vienna, Constantinople, Smyrna, Moscow, St. Petersburg. We find, for example, bound Gospels, varying in volume and decoration, prayer books, canonical books, etc. Outstanding among them is a special ritual book of clerical character printed in Ejmiatsin, the Holy See of the Armenian Supreme Patriarch, in 1778. On the ground floor of the Armenian school is the community library *Krasirats Yeghpayrutyun* ("Book-loving Brotherhood"), founded in 1883, which with its rich collection of books, periodicals, etc. has always been a center of literary, religious, and cultural life. The library and the Armenian Church Council of Plovdiv have launched on several occasions a campaign to collect printed publications in Armenian with the aim of enriching the fund for the so-called "literary heritage." Citizens willing to donate books and other materials in the Armenian language were encouraged to do so and received a donation certificate as an acknowledgment of their benevolence. The publications received were sorted by genre and subject and displayed in the library and in the crypt of the church, which houses a collection of special items. Initiatives such as this are important to help Armenians feel that they can concretely participate in the development of their library's holdings by sharing them for the benefit of all, and contribute to the preservation of their cultural heritage for future generations of Armenian readers.

---

23 The first two volumes appeared in 1885, one of them was published in Turkish, but with Armenian letters, and was the work *The Armenians and Eastern Rumelia.*

3.5. Literacy Levels and Language Attitudes

In Armenian culture, the written word is considered to have extraordinary power, and it is often seen as the most appropriate venue for linguistic action, including any kind of language planning. However, the other side of the coin with respect to writing is the issue of reading. In my experience in Plovdiv, I have found that only a minority of people are actually capable of reading texts written in the Armenian alphabet. Among the older generations, the language is still used extensively orally, but that does not mean that they can decipher it in its written form. Talking to my older interlocutors, a lively group of female pensioners who used to meet every Tuesday, I discovered that many of them have forgotten the language. However, there were also interesting exceptions represented by individuals particularly devoted to written culture and who, in order to maintain their reading skills in this alphabet, forced themselves to read Armenian texts as often as possible and attend the Armenian Evangelical Church, where reading Armenian texts, along with singing, occupies a dominant place (personal interview to Mrs. Srpuhi, October 2010). One woman told me that she made many efforts not to forget the alphabet she held so dear: she went to the school library (which is open only once a week, on Sundays in conjunction with the liturgy in church) to borrow the classics of Armenian literature she loved the most and read them in the evening before going to bed. Given the low level of Armenian literacy in this community, it seems obvious that the discourse on the role of written language in preserving Armenian identity in Plovdiv has nothing to do with the actual literacy skills of its members. The point is to explain how the rhetoric about the importance of Armenian writing is constructed and disseminated by local elites through the culture of writing itself, and how it succeeds in engaging even those who cannot read the language in a discourse of unity. Many members of the diaspora possess limited or no literacy skills in Armenian, a fact they deeply regret. Nevertheless, they participate in practices of community self-representation that highlight the prestige of Armenian writing. Through the local press, this prominence of the Armenian alphabet spreads to all levels of society and proves to be a strategy of identity remembrance linked to the ethnic survival of Armenian identity in the face of the great challenges of destiny, especially the Genocide. This is a way of celebrating Armenian particularity, conferring visibility to it in the face of the "significant Others"[24] within and outside the community. In everyday practice, however, the relationship with the Armenian alphabet is actually ambivalent because it often fails and can cause frustration: different forms of reappropriations of writing practices emerge, both socially and individually. For example, one of the activities that allow a relationship with the Armenian alphabet is attending the Armenian liturgy at the local Evangelical Church. In 2010, this was much more popular than the Apostolic Church, and the reason for this, according to my informants, was the fact that there is a direct contact with the texts in Armenian and not in *grabar*, the classical Armenian language. During the liturgy in the Evangelical Church, I noticed that the vast majority of people were predictably very old, but most importantly, not everyone was able to really read the texts that the priest pronounced. Many kept making mistakes while reading and singing, but no one seemed to care. I also joined in the chanting choir, trying to pronounce the Armenian letters as best I could, and I realized how important it was for those present to be together and relate to the Armenian written language collectively.

The Armenian writer Hovannes (Oncho) Mikaelian commented on this issue and assured me that he was doing a lot for the language, for example, by visiting the two Armenian churches to slowly get used to the language. The good thing about the Evangelical Church, in his opinion, was that everyone there was forced to read from the books and actively participate in the pronunciation of the language. Writing, on the other hand, was a "different thing," a huge challenge: he had tried for a long time to relearn the language in order to be able to write something in Armenian, which, of course, was not easy, and hoped to be able to do so one day (personal interview with Oncho Mikaelian, November 2010).

---

24 The term "significant Others" is used in social psychology to refer to those individuals who are of sufficient importance in a person's life to influence his or her feelings, behavior, and sense of self. It can be used at the "macro level" in the context of ethnopsychology or "national psychology."

However, the same writer in a later conversation confirmed the possibility of being Armenian outside the use of the Armenian language in the diaspora. Such view challenges the ascriptive traditionalist identity which sees the competence in the Armenian language as one of the basic preconditions of "being Armenian":

> Every Armenian in the world who writes, writes as an Armenian, in whatever language he or she expresses his or her thoughts: therefore, one speaks of an Armenian writer and not of a writer in Armenian. Language barriers are determined for each person by his or her destiny: I could not, unfortunately, learn to write in Armenian as I would have wished, because of the difficult life that forced me to work very hard and have little time for this language, but that does not change the fact that I feel fully Armenian. (Personal interview with Oncho Mikaelian, November 2010)

Despite his age (he was in his late 70s at the time of my first fieldwork), the writer made an effort to actively study and constantly develop his Armenian literacy skills, because he wanted to access texts written in this language. While thinking retrospectively, I can admit that, in a way, I myself have built my relationship with this Armenian community according to the "traditionalist" and ascriptive views on Armenian identity. Indeed, my aim was to be recognized as part of the "in-group" (Turner, Brown, & Tajfel 1979) from the beginning, mainly because of my dual plan to study the community and the written language, as an intention that was expressed to them and elicited praise and admiration. This is probably why people considered me "one of them" and made sure that I was involved in community life in various ways, trying to help me as much as possible with my work. Moreover, whenever I mentioned the topic of my research more or less explicitly, or sometimes even without doing so, people would put in my hands books or journals or other forms of written Armenian culture they possessed to show the extent to which this was part of their daily lives. These publications were often in Armenian and Bulgarian, sometimes also trilingual (Armenian-Bulgarian-English) as in the case of a book about a famous musician who lived in Plovdiv. In some homes, I could notice the presence of magazines in Armenian coming from other countries of the diaspora, such as those distributed free of charge by the Evangelical Church, which promote a "diasporic" evangelistic awareness that unites all Armenians around the world. It should be noted here that in Plovdiv, contrary to expectations, and as is further discussed in Chapters 5 and 6, most publications by Armenians are in Bulgarian. The presence of the Armenian language is greater in the periodical press (but still at a lower percentage than in Bulgarian), while the books are almost all in Bulgarian. However, this does not change the fact that the symbolic function is performed and maintained: even if the alphabet is not used practically as a writing medium, it survives as a recurring theme, as a sign of a tradition that is ever influential in its redundant visuality.

4. The Symbolic Cultivation of Identity in Education

Abstract: This chapter deals with the school domain and examines the symbols, narratives, and ideologies conveyed to children attending the local Armenian school and the Saturday classes organized by the diaspora organization, AGBU. The specificity of the lessons' contents is analyzed in relation to the emotional aspects of language preservation and the transmission of cultural memory. Furthermore, this chapter addresses the assimilation challenges faced by young Armenian adults in Plovdiv and discusses the issue of Western Armenian as an endangered language.

Keywords: Tutunjyan Armenian School, Armenian language classes, symbols of the Armenian nation, Armenian alphabet, Armenian as an endangered language

4.1. The Tutunjyan Armenian School from Its Origins up to Today

The issue of language acquisition and school education provides an opportunity to analyze not only the direct connection between student and teacher through the relationship to the "mother tongue" and its alphabet but also much broader questions about the ways in which an endangered language can be sustained in a diasporic context, the effectiveness of symbols in creating a shared collective memory, and the traditionalist ideological discourse associated with Armenian identity (Tchilingirian 2018). From an anthropological point of view, writing is understood as "more than a mere skill" (Papen & Barton 2010: 8): it is an activity with deep sociocultural implications, and it is the meaning attached to it that we wish to examine. In the case of the Armenian community, as already mentioned, a large part of the symbolic activity is mediated by the written culture and therefore, in analyzing its functioning, it is appropriate to try to trace the paths of its diffusion, starting from its place of origin, namely the school.

As mentioned earlier, until 1944 the children of the Armenian community in Plovdiv were educated in two independent institutions: the Viktoria and Krikor Tutunjyan School, the only one that still exists today, and the Mekhitarist School, which ceased its operation when the communist authorities ordered its closure due to its religious structure. The Tutunjyan School in Plovdiv is one of the oldest schools in the city and was founded in 1834, thanks to the Tutunjyan benefactors, a wealthy tobacco merchant couple. Its initial name was "Vartanants."[25] In the beginning, only boys were taught in the Vartanants Armenian School, according to the patriarchal understanding of the time. Only after the middle of the 19th century, in 1866, the girls' section of the school was opened.

As mentioned in Chapter 2, the school has gone through several historical phases, corresponding to the different political periods of the country. After an initial phase of functioning within the Ottoman sphere, characterized by margins of autonomy for minorities (including the existence of Greek and Armenian schools), education underwent changes after the Bulgarian Unification (1885), and the adoption of the new Tarnovo Constitution, especially in terms of modernization. The main subjects taught were as follows: Armenian language, Bulgarian language, French language, arithmetic, geometry, history of religion, singing, drawing, and calligraphy. Some of these were taught in Armenian with textbooks from Constantinople, the rest in Bulgarian. Later, textbooks in Armenian by native Armenian authors were used instead—anthologies, vocabularies, etc.— and the history and geography of Armenia were also adopted as subjects (Papazian-Tanielian 2016: 197). In addition, other activities such as drawing and singing were conducted in Armenian, as well as calligraphy, which has always played an important role in Armenian culture.

It was not until the 1920s that the students, who until then had been divided between two different buildings—one for boys and one for girls— found themselves in a single mixed Armenian school. It was also at this time that new subjects such as physics, chemistry, mathematics, history, and Bulgarian geography were introduced. In the school year 1925–1926, the school provided instruction up to the seventh grade and was recognized as a primary school with a junior high school. In the interwar period, education was characterized as democratic and independent of political divisions within the Armenian community. In terms of its importance to

---

25 In honor of historical Armenian hero Vartan Mamikonian.

the Armenian diaspora, no school in any city in the Balkans equaled the Tutunjyan Armenian School: all other institutions together had barely the same number of Armenian children. At this time, the city's Armenian minority was "a conglomerate of refugees from all parts of Turkey and some locals" (Vetsigian 2014: 109), and this was reflected in the composition of the pupils enrolled in the school. On the south side of the churchyard, on the site of the old Armenian school, a three-storey building of the new Armenian school was constructed in 1943–1944.

During the years of World War II, until 1944, the Tutunjyan Armenian School managed to preserve its autonomy from the ideologies that influenced Bulgaria, both fascism and communism. However, when the Communist Party came to power, the domestic policy toward the country's ethnic minorities also changed. First, the curricula were modified to include Marxist ideology in the textbooks, and eventually even the name of the school was changed after the Armenian-born communist official Stepan Shahumian, whose bust was placed on a pedestal in the courtyard of the school complex, together with a marble slab in his honor. However, the most impactful change in this initial period was that on the teaching of the Armenian language, with the introduction of the Eastern Armenian variant instead of the Western one, in accordance with the Soviet Union's directives. In 1976, the Communist Central Committee decreed the closure of the Tutunjyan School in Plovdiv, a fact that members of the community still remember with bitterness, as in this letter from a former student on the occasion of the celebrations for the school's 160th anniversary:

> I remember the anxious excitement that accompanied us when we first began to learn our maternal Armenian alphabet (...) What a pity that the closure of the school in 1976 deprived hundreds of children of the opportunity to be taught in their mother tongue, as it happened to my daughter and son, for example. Today I am grateful to and proud of (...) the Armenian school that taught me to write, read and speak in the mother tongue and helped me to love and be connected with our multi-secular culture. Garo Baltayan. (Tutunjyan 1994: 35)

Since the 1990s, following the democratic reforms in Bulgaria according to the *Convention on the Rights of Minorities*, mother tongue education has resumed in the Armenian minority School in Plovdiv, the only school in the whole of Bulgaria where education in Armenian is compulsory: in the other schools in Sofia, Varna, and Burgas, there is only optional education in this language. The date of September 16, 1990, when the school was able to resume its operations, is engraved in the memory of the entire community as a historic moment of the reappropriation of an institution that was fundamental to its survival as a specific linguistic and cultural identity. Just before the celebrations, a large fresco was painted on the main wall inside the building, which one passes to reach the second floor and enter the classrooms, depicting Meshrop Mashtots holding the alphabet board he invented in his hands. After the long interruption of all educational processes, the new Armenian generations faced many problems related to the resumption of schooling: the main difficulty was the lack of sufficient Armenian-speaking staff.[26] At this point, teachers established spontaneous contacts between the various cities and, through connections with the diaspora in the other countries where the schools existed without interruption, obtained the materials necessary to carry out the lessons. The textbooks came mainly from Syria, Lebanon, Italy, and Greek Cyprus. The materials were adapted to the programs of the Bulgarian schools so that they would be consistent with those of the parallel schools in the country. Thanks to the support of a prominent family of Armenian descent in the United States, personal contacts of the president of the Armenian General Benevolent Union (AGBU) in Plovdiv, and cooperation with the coordinator of educational programs at AGBU headquarters in New York, textbooks in Armenian were obtained for pupils in grades one through seven. The next step was to provide special rubric notebooks to help the children to learn to write in the Armenian language.

Currently, the Office of the High Commissioner for Diaspora Affairs sends textbooks and other educational materials to this institution annually, and efforts are underway to create a unified textbook in Western Armenian for all diaspora communities (Arakelyan 2015:10). The school has a few hundred children enrolled and covers seven school years (primary and middle school combined); it is highly regarded in Bulgaria for its work with the pupils, and it can sometimes be difficult to find a place

26 At the time of my fieldwork at the school in 2010, for example, teacher Malvina Manoukyan, originally from Yerevan, had been living in Bulgaria for about 30 years.

for the first year (personal interview with Viržinija Garabedyan, February 2010). This school represents a multiethnic model of coexistence, because the students who attend it are not only of Armenian origin but also Bulgarians, Roma, and even Turks: "They learn our language, sing Armenian songs, light candles in the Armenian church, and there is hope that in a few years perhaps these very children will cooperate in the solution of Armenia's historical problems" (personal interview with Malvina Manoukyan, September 2010).

Today, many subjects are taught: history, geography, mathematics, physics, music, and, above all, four languages from the first year of school: Armenian, Bulgarian, English, and Russian (the latter only in some sections). The Armenian School is a public school, and all its activities comply with the guidelines of the Bulgarian Ministry of Education.

The Viktoria and Krikor Tutunjyan School is located in a common area at the foot of Nebet Tepe hill, together with the church complex, the House of Culture, and the Krasirats Community Center: this area represents the center of the religious, enlightened, and cultural life of Armenians in the city, both in the past and today, and fits naturally into the diverse life of the city.

Nevertheless, one of the differences with the past, about which the members of this community often complain, is the fact that the so-called *armenska mahala* ("Armenian neighborhood") has been lost as an organizational form of the urban community: originally, until about 1900, Armenians inhabited the area of the historic city adjacent to the community core, where the school, church, library, etc. are located. With the arrival of refugees after 1922, they were mainly housed in a neighborhood not far away, so sending their children to the Armenian school remained the most obvious and easiest solution for everyone. However, in the course of the last decades, the residential development has shifted a lot and people now live even further away from the center of the community, so it has become more and more difficult to reach the school every morning: as a result, some Armenian children can no longer attend it. It is the aspiration and wish of the entire school collective that fewer and fewer children of Armenian origin remain excluded from this school, but the enrollment of the child in the Armenian school is a matter that also depends on the Armenian consciousness of the parents. In this regard, a positive role is played by both young people and adults who are active in the various Armenian organizations that promote Armenian identity through different sociocultural initiatives such as dancing groups, theater groups, etc.

4.2. Symbols of the Armenian Nation in Teacher Manoukyan's Lessons

When I first visited Plovdiv in 2010, much of the work in the field of Armenian literacy stemmed from the efforts of formidable teacher Malvina Manoukyan, a true pillar of the Armenian community in Plovdiv. Indeed, her commitment to teaching the Armenian language at the Tutunjyan School and, on a voluntary basis, at the so-called Saturday School was tireless. Furthermore, her method of allowing children to be in direct contact with the Armenian language through the learning of theatrical cues facilitated the acquisition of the language by the pupils. The cultivation of a sense of Armenianness in the children was definitely her strength together with the motivation to look for attractive methods against the assimilating risks of globalization and the ever-increasing penetration of the Internet into their lives. In the regular school curriculum, Armenian language classes are limited to a few hours per week and are the only ones that deal with Armenian culture. Parallel to the acquisition of writing and reading skills, the children are also exposed to topics of Armenian literature, folklore, history, geography, and nature: thus, it is a very intensive teaching for them. It must also be emphasized that these pupils are exposed to very different stimuli than children in other countries where only one alphabet is learned: they have to deal with at least three writing systems, Bulgarian Cyrillic, Armenian, and Latin for English, as well as Russian Cyrillic, which differs from Bulgarian by some additional special characters: in what constitutes an impressive multigraphic context. However, pupils are not isolated from the world around them: children mainly attend Bulgarian lessons about Bulgarian history and culture. Facts from Armenian history are often compared with analogies from Bulgarian history, and in this way the perception of Armenia becomes more accessible. As for the difficulties in teaching Armenian in schools, phonetics is certainly the most common problem. The tasks incumbent on teachers are very important and require joint meetings and comparisons between different bodies of teachers in order to solve the various challenges: every two years, a general meeting on the teaching methods for Armenian is organized, with the participation of specialists from Armenia. The composition of the classes is very diverse in terms of initial knowledge of this language: there are those who know it very well because they may hear it in their families, those who hardly speak it, those who know it only in the Eastern variant because they are children of recent immigrants from the new Republic of Armenia, and those who do not speak it at all but learn it even though they are Bulgarians.

The desire of teachers is to design instruction that not only teaches the concepts necessary for learning but also is attractive in content to engage the students' attention in a discourse that often extends beyond the school domain. As far as literacy is concerned, among the different learning environments, the field of writing is the most formalized in a society (Cardona 1981: 85): the most obvious reason for this is that writing is a form of highly praised knowledge that must be taught conservatively. Although the introduction of modern technologies changes the situation considerably, this statement proves especially true for minorities living in a different majority language context. Students must learn to write and read the particular writing system with extreme precision, as this is the first crucial step that introduces them to the knowledge conveyed through the written word.

From the very first lesson I attended with Teacher Manoukyan, I was very impressed with the way she conveyed respect and interest for this script, commenting with phrases like this: "The letters of this alphabet have been decorated with the most diverse ornaments throughout our history, which have also inspired numerous artists: therefore, you too must learn to write them very well!"

During the lessons, the children took turns at the blackboard, where they learnt to write each letter of this peculiar alphabet correctly with the help of a special table drawn with chalk, which resembles the lines of the musical pentagram. One of the most important lessons at the beginning of the school year is the one that focuses precisely on Mesrop Mashtots, the inventor of the Armenian alphabet. During the year when I also attended the lessons with the children, I was able to analyze in detail how the so-called "ideology of writing" linked to Armenian identity and Armenian collective memory was taught by the teacher in the school, in this case, Mrs. Malvina Manoukyan.

A child, about 8 years old, is asked to say in a few words in Armenian who Mesrop Mashtots is:

Child: "He is the father of Armenian writing, he invented the Armenian alphabet".

Teacher: "How many letters of the alphabet did he invent and which letters did he not invent?"

Child: "There are 36 letters, and the O and the F were not invented by him".

Teacher: "What does Mesrop Mashtots mean to Armenians?"

Child: "He is the first teacher".

Teacher: "But where is the word *our*? He is *our* first teacher..."

The teacher wants him to emphasize the possessive adjective our what he left out before. The questioning continues and the teacher again addresses the child directly in Armenian:

Teacher: "Now I want you to tell me how he invented the alphabet."

The child does not understand, and the teacher repeats the question, this time in Bulgarian, and adds: "I want you to tell me 'with love'".

The child says it in Armenian: "sirov."

Then, the teacher turns to everyone: "And why with love, children... Because if Mesrop Mashtots had not invented the Armenian alphabet, would we have all our Armenian writers?" The children answer in chorus: "No!"

Teacher: "That's right... We would not have had our Armenian literature and you would not be here now learning it with me in school..." The teacher begins to question another child.

Teacher: "Tell me something else about Mesrop Mashtots."

Child: "He translated so many books into Armenian".

Teacher: "Yes, because he is the one who invented those letters! Now I want to tell you something special: on the second Saturday of October, we celebrate Translator's Day. Because after Mesrop Mashtots invented these letters, his followers started translating into Armenian...Until then everything was written with Greek letters... And do you know what was the first book that Armenians translated when they finally had their alphabet? What would you translate?" The children answer impatiently and one child says: "I would write a story first". Another child replies: "I would write a book about language, about words... instead". Various answers follow, until the teacher says: "No... the first book was the Bible". "Aaaaaaaaaaaahhh!!! Of course!!!" say the children all together.

Teacher: "And who is this gentleman up here? Do you know Movses Horenatsi? He is a follower of Mesrop Mashtots who wrote the history of Armenians...Listen, in the year 405, Mesrop Mashtots invented the alphabet and then Movses Horenatsi wrote our first history, from the beginnings to the year 405, this crucial date. He collected legends, verses, texts, folk works..."

A little girl interrupts: "Something similar to what Paisii Hilendarski did for Bulgaria with his 'History of the Bulgarian People'!"

And the teacher answers: "Bravo, just like that... You see how close we Armenians are to the Bulgarians... Remember Movses Horenatsi, whom they call the father of Armenian history."

The lesson continues: "Today we also have grammar. I want to remind you that in Armenian the small letters of Mesrop Mashtots I and V together, when they are in the middle of the word, are read like the single character "Ю" ("Yu") in Bulgarian, while when they are at the end, they are pronounced as "IV". "But how are we going to learn this?" ask the children anxiously. "You guys will be fine, do not worry about it".

The teacher comes to me and comments on this: "They have to learn with love, because it's a difficult language, they cannot do it if you do not stimulate them, it must become an activity they want, an activity they love... Today they write down six words and learn them... and so every time." At the end of the class, homework is written on the blackboard exclusively in Armenian. It will be like this every time. The children understand almost entirely what the sentences mean, what the assignment is, but at home they have to make another effort to decipher them correctly, to be sure they are doing the exercise correctly. "And most importantly, practice at home to be able to tell the story of Mesrop Mashtots in Armenian!"

The example of this lesson about the father of Armenian writing shows how the teacher provides her students with the basics of reading and writing the alphabet but, more importantly, introduces a broader discourse in which the writing tradition and its relevance to the Armenian condition are essential elements, re-actualized in the diaspora perspective. The figure of Mesrop Mashtots is celebrated and humanized by the "love" with which he created this particular alphabet for the Armenian people; furthermore, he was the first teacher of Armenians, and thus, every teacher cannot help but refer to him as the supreme role model and feel especially legitimized in their activity. This also results in an interesting valorization and resignification of the contemporary figure of the Armenian language teacher in the collective Armenian consciousness: a kind of essential link in the chain that starts with God, who revealed the letters of the alphabet to Mesrop Mashtots and which connects to those who strive to spread his work in today's Armenian diaspora.

4.3. Myths of Collective Belonging at the Saturday School's Classes

In the Armenian school, learning ethnocultural information on Armenian identity goes hand in hand with the efforts to understand the Armenian language, which is used to convey this same knowledge. By virtue of the work carried out by the teacher, the children of Armenian origin begin to understand for the first time that they belong to a nation that has overcome numerous challenges in its centuries-long history and still exists with a distinct cultural and linguistic identity. The cultural tradition composed of myths and symbols can act on the feelings of identity of the children, fortified by the means of education, thus forming the fertile ground for the dissemination of the traditional cornerstones of Armenian collectivity. "The Church is our father, but the language is our mother," Armenians often say. Literacy acquisition in the mother tongue is a key factor for this, and Armenians value it highly. In fact, one very often hears the opinion that those who do not know the language and cannot read Armenian history and literature in the original are not real Armenians, (personal interview with new Armenian school director S. T., September 2010).

When meeting adult members of this community, it is very common for them to outwardly express their love for the Armenian school. In fact, letters from alumni are published in community newsletters and media, in which feelings related to learning Armenian are described:

> I am especially grateful to the teachers who taught me to read and write in my mother tongue, so that I could feel like a true Armenian anywhere in the world. And now, after so many years since I crossed the threshold of the Armenian school, I feel as if I have set my foot on a small piece of motherland, and I have

kept in my heart a small corner with cherished memories that belong only to the Armenian school. Seta Baltayan. (Tutunjyan 1994: 32)

In addition to regular Armenian school classes, another important context of language acquisition is the so-called "Saturday school," which constitutes an integrant part of the life of the Armenian community in Plovdiv, as elsewhere in the diaspora. Namely, the AGBU (Parekordzagan) organization, linked to the Armenian Church, promotes free extracurricular classes in Armenian language and culture for the children every Saturday morning, contributing to the "preservation and development of national consciousness" (Personal interview with Malvina Manoukyan). These classes are attended not only by the children living in Plovdiv but also by those coming from other small towns nearby. On average, about twenty children between the ages of 5 and 12 are enrolled each year. The Saturday classes are held in the AGBU Club, a small space outside the walls of the Armenian community complex that is regularly used for various social gatherings, including those organized by the Armenian youth, the female pensioners, etc. The annual program of Armenian Studies at the Saturday School includes topics from history, literature, and mythology. Some important dates in Armenian history are remembered and celebrated during special lessons: for example Vartanants, the day of the battle against the Persians led by the hero Vardan Mamikonian (see Ferrari 2016b: 7), the day of the beginning of the Genocide (April 24), and the Translator's Day (second Saturday of October). During the 2010-2011 school year, I had the opportunity to participate also in these lessons, which were then taught by the same teacher Malvina Manoukyan. Below is a brief description of the first Saturday School class that took place in October 2010.

Children who had already participated in the previous year's class read verses in Armenian to the audience, enthusiastically shouting "Im anush Hayastan" – "My sweet Armenia":

Teacher Manoukyan guides them and makes each of them declaim sentences in Armenian, explaining that "each child fills the colorful mosaic of the Armenian word with their recitation." She explains to those present that her method is to entertain the children mainly through theater, bringing the little ones even closer to their mother tongue and providing them with many reading exercises. She also introduces the novelty of the year, namely the introduction of an Armenian Studies course, where the participants will not only learn or improve the language but also acquire knowledge about many subjects related to "the rich culture of our ancient Armenia." "I will make sure that you learn the most important things, because Armenia is our homeland... You were born in Bulgaria, but our homeland is considered Armenia... You must be very literate, the most literate!"

The first lesson of the year is very important because it is the "initiation" lesson. It is called "The Symbols of Armenia."

M. M.: "The symbols of Armenia: what are they? What does the word mean? What does it mean, symbols of a country?"

Children: "Coat of arms, flag and anthem." Then an introduction to the topic through historical terms begins.

M. M.: "In 1918, after the First World War, Armenians manage to liberate a part of Armenia... And exactly in this part of the territory comprising Yerevan and Ejmiatsin, where our Church is located, the first free—remember these words well—free and independent Armenia is established. On May 28, Armenians can finally proclaim the Republic of Armenia as free and independent, free from Turks...Even though Yerevan was under Russians in the Eastern part...But now no one, neither Turks nor Russians, can rule it...After having founded it, we need a flag, a coat of arms, an anthem...Now we will see them. But first, tell me the colors of the Armenian flag."

A little girl says, "Garmir, gabuyd dziranakuyn", meaning red, blue, and orange.

The teacher goes on to ask: "And why "dziranakuyn" for orange? There was also the variant "narnchakuyn," but instead it was decided in recent years that it is better to use "dziranakuyn" in this context. Do you know why? It comes from the word "dziran"...What does "dziran" mean? Apricot... And why apricot? Because it is orange and therefore "dziran": apricot, and 'kuyn: color'. The apricot grows not only in Armenia, it is found all over the world...But we say that the homeland of apricot is Armenia, because wherever you find it, even in Bulgaria, it is never as delicious as in Armenia. I can tell you that the apricots in Armenia are very big, huge, like a peach...So big (showing it with her hands), and you can eat just one and feel full of it...They are incredibly tasty...We also use the inner apricot seeds and eat them."

In fact, next to the pomegranate, the apricot is one of the most revered fruits by Armenians, very often used for decorative purposes on book covers, newspapers, signs, and, of course, in culinary culture. It is very interesting that the teacher makes sure that we use the variant of the word orange, which is related to the word "apricot," instead of orange (dziranakuyn/narnchakuyn); this seems to me to be an example of how emotional attachment to certain symbols can even influence the choice of words to be used in the language. I have also noticed that Armenians have a great fondness for the orange color, perhaps because it is an unusual, almost unique, color in the flags of the world and is perceived as even more "native." I even participated in an evening organized by Armenian youth, where the dress code dictated that an orange—or better, apricot—garment be worn! Anyway, the meaning given to this color in the flag is different.

M. M.: "All colors of the flag have a meaning, they symbolize something. Red is blood....sunshine and blood...Blue is the sky and nature...Orange symbolizes wheat and diligence...Because our people are like that...Wherever we go, we work hard and manage to build our houses."

The children repeat: "garmir gabuyd dziranakuyn" and say in Armenian what each color means.

M. M.: "Bravo, then you are ready for the Olympics in Armenia". The teacher also tries to motivate the children with the prospect of the Armenian competitions in Yerevan, where only the best and most deserving pupils from the entire Armenian diaspora can participate. The teacher then introduces another very relevant topic, the Armenian national anthem, starting with a brief comparison with the Bulgarian anthem: "do any of you know the Bulgarian anthem?"

Children: "Yes...!"

M.M.: "What is it about?"

One child answers: "About the beauty of the Bulgarian nature."

M. M.: "That's right...But our hymn is about something else..."

Another child: "About the war!"

M. M.: "No, not about the war...You will find out now. The lyrics of the hymn were written by Mikayel Nalbandian, a writer, the title, as you know, is Our Fatherland, Mer Hayrenik."

Our Fatherland, free, independent/ That has lived for centuries,/ Is now summoning its sons/ To the free, independent Armenia./ Here is a flag for you my brother,/ That I have sewed / Over the sleepless nights,/ And bathed in my tears./ Look at it, tricoloured,/ A valuable symbol for us./ Let it shine against the enemy./ Let Armenia be glorious forever./ Death is the same everywhere,/ A man dies but once,/ Blessed is the one who dies/ For the freedom of his nation.[27]

The teacher recites the hymn with great feeling, translating and commenting on it, pointing out the words with which it begins—the same words she spoke at the start of the lesson—and the words with which it ends, which she considers the most important. A child asks why the flag was sewn at night, and the teacher explains that the night represents foreign domination and the pain the Armenian people have suffered over many centuries. Finally, she asks the children to memorize the lyrics of the hymn in Armenian, piece by piece. I will assess that the children will be able to recite the first two paragraphs in the very next lesson, and the hymn will accompany the pupils every Saturday. From the brief example in this class, one can ascertain the special way in which the teaching of the Armenian language and culture takes place during Saturday classes. In this context, a lexicon that enriches the children's vocabulary is combined with illustrations, stories, and other stimuli that facilitate the memorization of new concepts. By moving from literature to traditions, folklore, historical, and geographical aspects of the "Motherland," a multifaceted approach to all the important traditional elements associated with Armenian identity is achieved.

The rhetoric used in schools (as well as in the media) is extremely rich in symbolism and emotion, for this is indeed the way discourse of identity is conducted across all spheres of community life, advocating an essentialist form of collective expressions (Tchilingirian 2018). This should not be too surprising, because in order to affirm its existence and prevent assimilation, a diasporic community draws sustenance from these dynamic and repetitive practices of transcontextuality: they form the foundations of diasporic ontology. Each element mentioned refers back to something else, by approaching the form of the symbol: so perhaps while learning the

---

27 The words of the Armenian national anthem are adapted from a version of "The Song of the Italian Maiden" by poet Mikayel Nalbandian.

alphabet, the anthem, or a poem, a child can find the key to access broader meaningful knowledge placed in a transnational context of signification.

In the Saturday School of Plovdiv, as well as in the regular classes of the Armenian school, the ethnic and national symbols are used in their practical dimension as means of learning the Armenian language as well as on a "mythopoetic" level as elements related to discourses of Armenian identity, acquiring strategic importance for the creation of a specific emotional imaginary of belonging. The role of the teacher in the Armenian diaspora context acquires a special meaning as a "transmitter" of symbols. This figure also encourages children to recognize their own distinctiveness and to strive to preserve it by developing affection toward an "imaginary" homeland in which the Armenian collectivity finds its sense of unity and protection.

4.4. Language Challenges after Childhood

The issue of language use outside of school, especially in the everyday context of the family, is very complex, as it has always been in the lives of members of the Armenian diaspora in this city. Even today, in some cases, it is difficult to determine which language is spoken at home, whether Armenian or Bulgarian; bilingualism in the family context is a very common feature. However, since the Armenian language has a limited scope, the situation could be better described as diglossia: Bulgarian represents the "high" variety of the repertoire, because it is the national language, the language of the official and bureaucratic domain, while Armenian has more to do with the family and everyday sphere and very little with the institutional sphere (only in some activities promoted by associations within the community, but marginally). The crucial point is that not all speakers of Armenian origin are proficient in the Armenian language; in fact, the percentage is very low, and those who speak it, especially among the youth, often have very "imperfect" knowledge and cannot be considered native speakers. There are many differences in their competences, and it is difficult to construct a pattern that fits all the cases represented in this diaspora.

In the social context outside the family, when people meet, it sometimes happens that they switch from one language to another: a few sentences are exchanged in Armenian, then they start speaking in Bulgarian. I have seen such examples of code-switching not only at the meetings of elderly pensioners but also at social events, where the evening on stage was presented first in Armenian and then in Bulgarian, or at the rehearsals for the performance of some plays in Armenian, where the people behind the scenes gave the hints in Bulgarian. I noticed the case of a boy who spoke Armenian very well but had a reading block toward the Armenian alphabet, so he used Bulgarian transliteration to help himself with reading the play. The explanation for this fact is that nowadays Bulgarian is used more often in everyday life, and besides, especially young people, including those who learned Armenian as their first language at home, say that they have a richer vocabulary in Bulgarian that enables them to express their thoughts and talk about a wide variety of topics, while in Armenian they feel they can only speak about a limited series of topics:

> Armenian was my first language, I learned it at home, and my brother and I had to learn Bulgarian when we started having non-Armenian friends... We were very young and did not really know how to communicate in Bulgarian, but little by little we learned it... Then, as I grew up, Armenian became more and more inappropriate for the vocabulary of modern life, because, for example, certain words like those for technology were not there, and so even in my mind Bulgarian gradually replaced Armenian, although I have not forgotten it, I use it in the family, but even there we often end up speaking in Bulgarian. (Personal interview with Gayane S., September 2010)[28]

The fact that Armenian proves to be unsuitable for the communicative needs of modern life is related to its presence in European contexts (including Bulgaria) as a language of the diaspora: Armenian is a family language, not a language of society. This was not the case in the Ottoman Empire, for example, in Constantinople, where there were Armenian producers in all sectors: they were often the best and therefore their language prevailed, at least within the community (Kılıçdağı 2010). In today's diaspora, only those who actively read Armenian books, have the Armenian satellite channel, or watch news and videos on the Internet acquire a richer

---

28 In this case, learning of the second language—Bulgarian—the dominant language in Plovdiv's external social context, came at the expense of the first language, Armenian.

vocabulary, but most young people are rather passive in this regard and do not significantly expand the scope of this language. I am aware of only isolated cases of young Armenians from Plovdiv pursuing academic careers in Armenian Studies at Sofia University, the only institution in all of Bulgaria where this course is offered. The community, through the AGBU organization, advertises this study opportunity in its newspaper and offers financial assistance for tuition fees to those who wish to enroll in the program.

When thinking about the future of the Armenian language in the diaspora, it is also important to mention the situation of mixed marriages, which is relatively new and not yet so widespread. Many people have told me that until about 40 years ago, it was not permissible for an Armenian to marry a member of another ethnic group because the goal of the community was to maintain a certain "purity" and continuity in the transmission of Armenian culture, including the language. Today there is lesser and lesser opposition to this practice, but one of my older informants lamented the loss of these good old traditions, was very disappointed that her grandson had married a Bulgarian, and hoped with all her heart that her granddaughter would find an Armenian husband. It is therefore appropriate to ask whether the children of mixed marriages forget their dual origins, because it is true that the Armenian language is not spoken very often in such families and it tends to be very difficult for a Bulgarian to learn Armenian (Tavityan 2021:184–185). There are, however, also exceptions: in some cases of mixed couples that I have been able to observe, the Armenian identity of the family seemed to be even strengthened. A young informant with a Bulgarian father and an Armenian mother grew up with a strong sense of her Armenian identity and was also very involved in the community: she was a journalist at the AGBU newspaper and worked in an Armenian company. She attended the Armenian school as a child and, during the time of my first fieldwork, was trying to catch up on her written language skills through private classes and courses taught by volunteers, which was very challenging given her busy schedule. Another case was that of a mixed couple in their 20s; she had come from Yerevan many years earlier, and he was a Macedonian-Bulgarian. They had been married for a few years and were among the pillars of the young generation involved in the community. He spoke a few words of Armenian. They had been in Armenia on a cultural trip. The Armenian identity was clearly the dominant one, culturally, between the two of them.

Many people in their 20s admitted that their interest in the Armenian homeland had aroused quite late, namely only a few years earlier, and was also related to what they read about their homeland, especially in Armenian newspapers. The interest had been latent for long and had only developed as they matured and became aware of their role in the community, in a process leading to resistance to assimilation to the Bulgarian context. The "critical" years for identity, especially given the lack of opportunity to further study language or culture in school, are therefore the teenage years. After the end of the middle school years (when children are 13–14 years old), they have less opportunities to participate in the community, and many times do not feel the need to do so. This is unfortunate because during these years the language that was painstakingly learned at school gradually falls into oblivion, especially in its written form. As a result, awareness of belonging to a specific and distinct culture does not usually emerge until a few years after graduation from high school. At that time, young people may begin to read the Armenian press and actively participate in community initiatives.

Thus, in the individual history of approaching Armenian written culture, after childhood (when school establishes contact with Armenian writing), and after the critical period of adolescence (when there is no Armenian high school), the next meaningful context is that relating to the press, which is crucial for the formation of the Armenian sense of identity. Moreover, among the journalists of one of the two Armenian newspapers in Plovdiv, the AGBU biweekly *Parekordzagani Tzain*, we also find alumni of the Tutunjyan School, as part of a special program to involve young people in the newspaper's editorial work. In an interview, school director Viržinija Garabedyan defined this as a real success—a confirmation of the great goal of this school—to educate children in the Armenian spirit. This is seen as a seed from which the mature and self-aware fruit of active participation in the discourse on Armenian identity can grow.

Sometimes, a desire may arise in young people to regain their language skills at the written level. The HOM Association or Women's Charity (affiliated with the Red Cross) takes care of this by organizing free weekly Armenian language classes for young adults. In 2010, I had the opportunity to attend some classes with some of my peers (aged about 23 to 26) and could witness the good will both on the part of the teacher, an elderly lady full of enthusiasm, and on the part of the students, committed to working on the difficult grammar exercises. A 25-year-old informant commented on her participation:

> I really enjoy coming to Mrs. Nersisyan's classes. I started about three months ago because I wanted to find a way to overcome my block in written language, and I am doing very well, even though I am a little embarrassed because I still have trouble reading out loud... And imagine, every now and then the teacher even makes us read Armenian epic texts, which are very beautiful! (Personal interview with A. Z., October 2010)

Mrs. Nersisyan's classes were indeed very inspiring and well designed, and I also attended some of them in 2010, trying to improve my Armenian language skills, feeling connected to young people like me, with whom I shared somehow a feeling of Armenianness I wanted to develop.

4.5. Old and New Literacy Practices for an Endangered Language

Expanding the writing and reading contexts of a minority and diaspora language, enabling its use for new functions, and increasing its scope (especially in the case of the Internet and online communication) certainly has a positive impact on the community's self-image (Koulayan 2006) and on the ideologies that promote the preservation of the language. The danger that the language will be mastered lesser and lesser by the younger generation is real and obvious. This is a concern not only for the teachers in the schools but also for journalists and volunteers whose work seeks to improve this situation and provide the necessary means to stimulate and reactivate attention to the language. The results are good in that the efforts of the intelligentsia often meet with a sincere, participatory response from the wider audience, proving the vitality of a minority resisting assimilation. All initiatives promoted by the local intelligentsia are expressions of a strategy aimed at consolidating communal bonds through practices of identity-making, clinging to a common and somehow idealized heritage. This connects the specific diaspora of Plovdiv to "other times" and "other spaces," a fact which constitutes the biggest resource of the Armenian diaspora dimension. In this sense, the Plovdiv diaspora is connected at the same time to Yerevan and to the countries of the diaspora all over the world through a network of cultural links activated and embodied by the Apostolic Church and various Armenian associations, first and foremost the Armenian General Benevolent Union.

In the perspective of modernization, digitalization, and globalization, and in order to better meet the current needs of the Armenian diaspora, the so-called Armenian Virtual College was created at the international and transnational level, which aims to become "the leading online higher education institution in Armenian Studies with an educative outreach worldwide" (AVC website).[29]

This online platform has been used with great success in Saturday classes in Plovdiv for about five years, offering a fresh perspective to Armenian children who want to learn the language. In addition to language classes, the children also have access to courses on Armenian history, literature, music, architecture, and chess, as well as other cultural lectures with virtual tours of Armenia. In recent years, social media, especially Facebook, have played a crucial role in promoting written messages in Armenian aimed at all generations. Nevertheless, most young people on the Internet write Armenian with Latin letters, a phenomenon that could also be influenced by the fact that Bulgarian users also tend to write with the Latin rather than the Cyrillic script (Selvelli 2021: 251).

Many members of the Armenian community admit that the Armenian language of the diaspora in Plovdiv is an endangered language for the future younger generations, in the sense that the near future looks less promising. There is, however, hope that the acquisition of literacy at school can prevent this unlucky scenario from happening, allowing today's children to read the Armenian newspapers published in Plovdiv one day, along with other examples of written culture. Teacher Manoukyan commented as follows:

> They need to know how to write and read. Do you know what it means for these young children to attend this class? How much effort they have to put in to be able to read part of the newspaper in Armenian one day? This is a very important

---

29 https://www.avc-agbu.org/departments/armenian-language

question. In my classes I make sure that the children can read well and clearly without any problems. Will they be able to read newspapers in the future? I think so...For example, in class V there are two children who can already read a text that they have never seen before without any problems. Other two on the other hand are very weak, one is of mixed marriage background while the other has some problems... They do not know much about what we learn here in class... In class VII when they finish school they must be able to at least read, write and speak...But after that there is nothing...They are done with learning Armenian... (Personal interview with Malvina Manoukyan, November 2010).

The problem is that, while Armenian schooling makes a basic contribution to the preservation of the language, it is by no means sufficient, since it only covers the age group from 6 to 14. After that, no secondary school exists where teenagers can develop their language skills in Armenian. In fact, many people in their 20s lamented this lack, recalling how well they could write and read Armenian during their school years, and how after so many years, they have unfortunately lost the ability, or at least the spontaneity, to refer to the Armenian alphabet. In 2010, an exception was constituted by the group of "privileged" ones who were lucky enough to attend the prestigious Armenian High School in Cyprus. However, this was closed in 2005, depriving Armenians of an important educational institution. The challenge, thus, remains that of integrating practices of literacy in this language into everyday life, since young teenagers find themselves in a world where the actual use of written or spoken Armenian is very limited. Planning to support the writing and reading skills that these children have acquired is as important as the language initiation program. In this respect, the Internet is a dimension which could provide such opportunities—by facilitating, for example, communication with Armenians all over the world—along with the three-week summer camps in Armenia (called "Discover Armenia") organized annually by the AGBU and the other rich programs and initiatives of this international diaspora organization.

5. The AGBU Initiatives in Support of Language and Memory

Abstract: This chapter focuses on the role of the international diaspora organization AGBU/Parekordzagan in promoting positive attitudes toward the Armenian language and collective memory practices through both print media and social activities. I analyze the AGBU's bilingual (Armenian-Bulgarian) bulletin "Voice of Benevolence" (*"Parekordzagani Tzain"*) and discuss its ability to mobilize the community around genocide remembrance initiatives. Finally, I explain the relevance and currency of issues related to neighboring Turkey for this specific Armenian community.

Keywords: AGBU, *Parekordzagani Tzain*, post-memory of the genocide, collective memory, Armenian diaspora and Turkey

5.1. The Armenian General Benevolent Union (AGBU) in the Diaspora

As discussed in the previous chapter, the Armenian diaspora in Plovdiv, as well as all over the world, undoubtedly attaches great importance to promoting the teaching and learning of the Armenian language. Mastery of the Armenian language is seen by the promoters of a traditionalist view on identity as an essential tool for penetrating the deep roots of Armenian culture and familiarizing oneself with the heritage of this community (Gueriguian 1997: 137) which has experienced major survival challenges in its recent history. "And look, my son, wherever you are, wherever you go under this moon, even if you leave your mother out of your mind, never forget your Mother Tongue!" state the popular verses of poet Silva Kaputikyan[30] (see Abgarian 1997: 165). This notion, which links linguistic competence and Armenian identity, contrasts with the reality of today's Armenian diaspora, where only a minority of its members is actually fluent in the language, but nevertheless engages in activities and

---

30 From the poem "A word to my son", 1952.

practices that sustain diaspora life, culture, and connections within the community (Sahakyan 2021).

The diasporic organization AGBU (Armenian General Benevolent Union) or *Parekordzagan* ("charity" in Armenian) is the very core of cultural activities aimed at maintaining inner cohesion. It provides spaces for youth and elderly meetings and promotes language and culture through extracurricular classes, book publications, and issues the most popular newspaper of the community, the biweekly bulletin *Parekordzagani Tzain*. The AGBU, founded in Cairo in 1906 by Pasha Boghos Nubar, is the largest non-profit organization of the Armenian diaspora worldwide, coordinating various activities on the international level. After World War II, it moved its headquarters to New York, where it remains today. Its members form a network that includes more than twenty countries hosting relevant Armenian communities. They are usually influential and powerful Armenians who can provide their own resources by donating funds to the organization. From its inception, the founding idea of the organization was to preserve the Armenian identity through cooperation in the field of education, which is why activities in this area are purposefully promoted and supported.

The AGBU has its own channels in Bulgaria, where its branches were established already in 1910. During the 45 years of communist rule, the AGBU was dissolved and replaced by the Erevan Association, although it secretly managed to keep some of its activities alive. It resumed its regular activities in this country in 1991. Surprisingly, Bulgaria is today the country having the second highest number of AGBU branches (after the United States), located in the cities of Burgas, Dobrič, Haskovo, Plovdiv, Ruse, Silistra, Sliven, Sofia, Varna, and Yambol. The president of each city is elected every two years at a joint meeting of the local members. The main funds come from membership fees, the organization of charity concerts, dances, and theatrical performances and, occasionally, help comes from the headquarters in New York. Nowadays, activities have expanded, and support is not only for education but also for cultural activities. High-achieving students receive scholarships to continue their university studies, and children with outstanding artistic or musical abilities have the opportunity to receive financial support to attend special schools in Bulgaria or abroad.

In addition to the cultural and educational components of AGBU activities, there is also a strong interest in promoting discourse and collective memory of the Genocide among members of the diaspora and beyond. In this regard, the AGBU has a dual role, a political one (collective representation of the Armenian community) and a spiritual one (linked to the authority of the Armenian Apostolic Church).[31]

The AGBU stands out also as the primary actor capable of channeling the "post-memory" (Hirsch 2008) of the collective trauma of the Genocide. It actively works to transform family experiences and trauma into a transgenerational form of memory (Holslag 2018) embedded in a shared symbolic system of meaning and a powerful collective imaginary. The AGBU's work enables the later descendants of survivors to connect deeply with the injustices suffered by their ancestors and to identify fully with their suffering. This connection is reinforced by the continued refusal of the Turkish authorities and the majority of the Turkish public to acknowledge the reality of the Genocide. The activities and discourse supported by the AGBU promote the acceptance of a symbolic framework that is activated on certain occasions for interaction among community members. Commemorations are a necessary part of Armenian life, without which the acts of the perpetrators of the genocide would be legitimized. Armenians "who want to be ethical, are, so to say, doomed to commemorate," to such an extent that the survivors' descendants have a particular "post-genocide mode of being" (Seppälä 2016).

5.2. The AGBU Bilingual Bulletin *Parekordzagani Tzain* ("Voice of Benevolence")

The AGBU and its informative bulletin *Parekordzagani Tzain* are politically aligned with the historical Armenian party *Ramgavar*, which is closer to liberal principles, in contrast to the leftist view of the historical Armenian party *Dashnaktsutiun* expressed in the newspaper *Vahan* ("Shield" in

---

31 Another diaspora organization present in Plovdiv is the philanthropic and humanitarian Armenian Relief Society (H.O.M.), which nevertheless plays a marginal role compared to the powerful AGBU. For Armenian diaspora institutions worldwide, see Tölölyan 2000.

Armenian). The *Parekordzagani Tzain* saw the light of day in September 2004, and its articles reflect the principles of AGBU and inform its readers about initiatives at the local, national, and international levels. The editorial novelty in the context of the Bulgarian diaspora was received with great enthusiasm by the then AGBU World General President:

> I welcome the initiative of your branch, and especially the young people with whose help you will publish the newspaper, a first-time initiative aimed at reflecting the AGBU's activity before the Bulgarian society. At the same time, the Parekordzagani Tzain will give resonance to the interest in the preservation of the nation (...). The central leadership has a great interest in the needs of the Armenian community in Bulgaria and its activities. (Setrakian 2004: 2)

Similar enthusiasm was expressed by the Chairman of the AGBU branch in Plovdiv, Mr. Rupen Chavushyan, in his opening message published in the same first issue of *Parekordzagani Tzain*:

> Dear readers, before you is the first issue of the newspaper Parekordzagani Tzain, published by the Plovdiv branch of the charity organization Parekordzagan. It will strive to be our newspaper that will inform its readers about the problems of our daily life and what awaits us in the future. The newspaper will be published thanks to the direct help of young people who, with their work and courage, will inform us about important aspects of our present. In this regard, we hope for your support, dear reader. (...) Time will tell how successful we will be in the challenge of expanding the scope of information for our community (...). We sincerely believe that, in accordance with the ideals and values of Parekordzagan, our newspaper will act as a catalyst for charity and goodwill. (Chavushyan 2004: 1–2)

The *Parekordzagani Tzain* often publishes biographical articles about specific historical figures of Armenian origin whose works have contributed to the spread and development of Armenian culture in the world. Other typical articles deal with the history and life of Armenian communities in other countries of the world, in India, Egypt, Poland, and also in neighboring Romania. In addition, much attention is paid to the activities of AGBU members in Bulgaria, as well as throughout the diaspora: articles praising the value of their activities are published by others who are closer to and important to the Plovdiv community. This is an effective means of acknowledging the efforts of those who work for the benefit of the Armenian language and culture, which encourages the community through positive examples:

A nation remained alive after so much violence, fires and massacres, and yet pre-served their customs and culture. Now we, its descendants, have the duty to learn from its morals and dignity in order to survive as a people forever in the centuries to come, to carry on the songs and dances, the melodious Armenian language to the world. In 2004, Mrs. Arshavir received the Silver Medal for her contribution to the promotion of the ideas of Parekordzagan and the cultivation of our ethnic values and language. The lady has a music school and teaches Armenian songs to her singing students. Only 10% of them speak Armenian, but the difficult Arme-nian words flow like clear water, so expressive. (Parekordzagani Tzain 2004: 3)

Over the years, the newspaper was gradually expanded and is now published biweekly. Many columns appeared: one on literature; one on poetry; one on the AGBU's young professionals; one entitled "We are our values" on different Armenian cultural traditions; one on facts and events affecting the Plovdiv community, including trips to the Republic of Ar-menia and Turkey; one on Armenia and the worldwide diaspora (entitled "Spyurk"); and many others. As for the written language, this is predom-inantly Bulgarian, but there are always at least some articles in Armenian and most articles have a double title in Armenian and Bulgarian: thus, the visualization of the Armenian alphabet is a constant factor while reading this publication. Through the newspaper, Armenian readers have the op-portunity of feeling more connected to each other in relation to the tradi-tional values of Armenian identity and also have the chance of developing their own personal sense of belonging to the dimension of Armenianness. The *Parekordzagani Tzain* is a great success and has subscribers outside the country as well, Armenians from the wider diaspora, emigrants from Bulgaria, Canada, France, the United States, etc. It is with great pleasure that I, too, have subscribed to the newspaper, which I have been receiving for years in Italy—in paper form first and then in electronic form—helping the Armenian word travel from Plovdiv to new destinations.

Compared to the weekly *Vahan*, the *Parekordzagani Tzain* is much less concerned with issues of contemporary politics and is more inclined to write about events within the Armenian community of Plovdiv and Bul-garia and to describe the many activities of the AGBU worldwide. As Mrs. Hripsime Erniasyan, editorial chief of the newspaper explains in an inter-view: "Although sometimes we have to deal with some issues of Armenian politics, you can hear politics on TV or read it on the Internet; on the contrary, what is happening in Dobrich, for example, or what Armenians are doing in Burgas, that is something you cannot find anywhere else" (Personal interview with Hripsime Erniasyan, November 2010).

Through the employment of a wide range of symbolic elements in its contents, one gets the impression that this newspaper tends to privilege a historical dimension of "Armenianness": it appeals to the sense of belonging to a past dimension of the nation where time has, to some extent, stopped. Indeed, while the Republic of Armenia is somehow more focused on its present challenges, diaspora communities often tend to nourish themselves of pre-diasporic customs and social structures, interpreting their role as that of the custodians of a common national heritage (Aghanian 2007).

The newspaper *Parekordzagani Tzain* regularly organizes competitions to find journalists and collaborators from Plovdiv and the whole country, as well as correspondents from Burgas, Ruse, Stara Zagora, and Varna. Commitment to the Armenian cause is crucial for participation in the AGBU's activities. Furthermore, collaboration in the editorial work is a very effective way to involve young people in a tangible way and make them feel that they are useful to the community. The newspaper asks young members for their support and collaboration. In this way, young adults have the opportunity to learn the profession of journalism and to offer their translation skills from foreign languages (especially English). After many years, young people attended the Tutunjyan School are brought back into direct contact with the Armenian language by requiring them to engage in reading and writing activities in an "institutionalized" workplace at the newspaper headquarters, where this language plays a fundamental role. In this way, they are encouraged to regain the knowledge of Armenian that they (usually) abandoned after entering secondary school, where this is not taught.

As for the children, their "initiation practices" to the Armenian language and alphabet are particularly important in relation to this newspaper, which publishes columns specifically dedicated to them. For example, over the years, they had the opportunity to follow the stories of one of the greatest Armenian writers, Hovhannes Tumanyan (1869–1923): these were published exclusively in Armenian and written in a very simple language, which invited the children to read them—or have someone else read them—and wait for their continuation in subsequent issues. Sometimes there are also riddles and world puzzles, games with which the children (but not only them) can practice the Armenian language. For the older ones there are also jokes, proverbs, short entertaining stories, etc.

The work of the translators is considered indispensable by the staff of the newspaper *Parekordzagan Tzain*, because, thanks to them, Armenian books can be published in a Bulgarian edition, and besides, they are very often the ones responsible for the selection of material to be offered to the public. As mentioned, the policy of the publication is that a certain degree of bilingualism is always present, and thus we find texts in Armenian referring to the Diaspora and others in Bulgarian concerning the events of Armenians in this Balkan country. This Armenian newspaper from Plovdiv has the honor of landing also in the Matenadaran Library in Yerevan, which is considered the most important institution in the country for the preservation of Armenian written culture. For the journalists who work there, it is of great pride that it remains in the archive of the oldest temple of manuscripts in Armenia, where it is sent at their request. In addition, the paper is also sent to the Mayor in Sofia and to all institutions related to culture, art, and ethnic groups in Bulgaria, including several copies to the Sofia National Library "Saints Cyril and Methodius," that then further disseminates this publication in its other national branches.

5.3. Initiatives Commemorating the Armenian Genocide in Plovdiv

By reading through the pages of the *Parekordzagani Tzain*, one becomes aware of the central importance that this newspaper and the organization behind it attach to the topic of the Armenian Genocide. In general, the difficult issue of relations with Turkey and its denial of the Genocide is very present in the discussions of Plovdiv intellectuals and community representatives. This is particularly evident in the pages of the local press. The AGBU helps organize fundraising activities for the construction of monuments to the victims of the Genocide and mobilize resources for practical initiatives, as in the following 2015 announcement:

> On April 24, we celebrate the 100th anniversary of the Armenian Genocide! In this context, we are raising funds to commemorate this tragic anniversary, which we will express through various informative tools—billboards, banners, posters and more. We sincerely encourage everyone who is interested to support this noble initiative according to their possibilities. (Parekordzagani Tzain 2015: 1)

To mark the occasion, the AGBU branch in Plovdiv displayed the forget-me-not flower, a symbol chosen by the diaspora worldwide to commemorate the Genocide. Along with the flower, the following phrases were displayed: "I remember and I condemn. I remember and I demand. I live and I remember. I live and I demand." The symbol of the forget-me-not confirms that the existence of the Armenian diaspora is ontologically dependent on the memory of its past, that is, on the memory of the suffering and tragedy experienced by its ancestors. Genocide commemorations are held on April 24, the day of the first organized deportation of Armenian intellectuals from what was then Constantinople to the city of Ankara in 1915, which marked the beginning of the physical extermination of almost the entire Armenian population living in the historical territories of Western Armenia. The Armenian massacres have been recognized as "genocide" by twenty-nine countries and by various international organizations and institutions, including the United Nations (1985) and the Council of Europe (2001). In 2015, coinciding with the centenary of the beginning of the persecutions, the Bulgarian Parliament adopted a declaration recognizing the events, although it did not classify them as "genocide" but as "mass extermination of the Armenian people in the Ottoman Empire" (Kévorkian 2006: 251).[32] However, the municipalities of Plovdiv, Burgas, Ruse, Stara Zagora, and Pazardžik have officially recognized the Armenian massacres as "genocide" for several years, a fact which in some cases has led to tension in Bulgaria's relations with Turkey.[33]

In considering the patterns that perpetuate the memory of the Genocide in Armenian communities around the world, it is important to remember that official commemorations of this tragedy have only been taking place since the 50th anniversary of the event, in 1965. However, the memory of the Genocide has shaped the diaspora long before that date. The political

---

32 On this occasion, then Prime Minister Boyko Borisov had initially intended to use the Bulgarian term for "genocide"; however, in his ultimate declaration he did not do so and thus did not satisfy those who hoped for unequivocal recognition at the international level.

33 An example of this is the suspension of a project to establish a low-cost airline link between Plovdiv and the city of Bursa in Turkey following the recognition of the Armenian Genocide by Plovdiv's municipal council.

Figure 5.1. Wall Outside the Armenian School Tutunjyan Commemorating the 100th Years since the Armenian Genocide, in Armenian and Bulgarian [Credits: G.S.].

context (including Soviet-imposed restrictions on minority freedom of expression) and practical and psychological factors (such as the focus of the global diaspora's energies and resources on integration into their host countries) inhibited public discussion of the issue.

Since the 50th anniversary, Genocide survivors, together with their children and grandchildren, have finally been able to break the "wall of silence" that blocked the expression of their memories in the previous decades. For this reason, half a century later, many young Armenians became increasingly engaged in political activities and demonstrations, having been exposed in an intergenerational way to a cultural trauma that "left indelible marks upon their group consciousness, marking their memories forever, and changing their future identity in fundamental and irrevocable ways" (Hovannisian 1986: 113). Unsurprisingly, the specific pattern of functioning of the Armenian diaspora has been rooted in its continuous confrontation with the trauma of the 1915 Genocide. According to the famous Romanian-Armenian writer Varujan Vosganian, author of the novel

The Book of Whispers, memory has become "more important than both death and life" (Gaun 2014: 9–11). Its emotional effects extend far beyond the first generation of the survivors' descendants, proving that family memory can be reproduced and transmitted into the minds and hearts of much later generations. This is possible because individual stories, images, and narratives persist not only in the family domain, but also through affiliative forms of "post-memory" (Hirsch 2008)[34] and through more institutionalized, externalized examples of cultural memory (Assman 2008).

Plovdiv is a city particularly sensitive to Armenian history, as it is home to the largest Armenian community in Bulgaria. It is therefore not surprising that the celebrations on April 24 are always marked by a large turnout and great emotions.[35] The day usually begins with a memorial service at the Surp Kevork Armenian Apostolic Church, followed by a few minutes of silence in front of the large wooden cross (*khachkar*) located in the courtyard of the community complex between the church and the Tutunjyan Armenian School. Pupils usually recite poems dedicated to their ancestors who perished in the Genocide and honor the victims by laying flowers around the monument. Then, in the afternoon, members of the Armenian community and representatives of local Armenian organizations, along with Bulgarians, march down the city's main street waving the Armenian and Bulgarian flags. The commemoration ends in Plovdiv's central square, where a statement is read calling on Turkey to recognize as "genocide" the crimes committed against Armenians during World War I.[36] As is well known, the essence of commemoration is participation, the coming together of people to honor its object of memory. The annual march on April 24 is a true *lieu de mémoire* (Nora 1984: 29) intended to affirm a specific memory, and is a symbolic collective practice that shows

---

34 This concept has already been employed in many works dealing with the memory of the Armenian Genocide. See, for example, Gulesserian 2015, Fırat Şannan, Muti, Gürpınar & Özkaya 2017.

35 Commemorations also take place in some of the other major cities of the country, including Sofia, Varna, Silistra, Ruse, and Pleven.

36 In 2018, the day ended with the screening of the recent documentary on the Armenian Genocide, entitled "Izkorenjavane" ("Extirpation"). The film was made by a Bulgarian director, Kostadin Bonev, in 2017. It was screened simultaneously in Plovdiv and in several other Bulgarian cities.

the unity and continuity of the community (Selvelli 2018). As mentioned earlier, the weeks leading up to April 24, 2015, were filled with news of initiatives related to the commemoration of the Genocide, as it happened among all Armenian communities worldwide (Gül 2018). One of these initiatives was a play directed by Evelina Nikolova and performed by the Armenian Children's Theater School in Plovdiv, based on Vosganian's work *The Book of Whispers*.

The venue for this commemorative event was the well-known *Kuklen Teatăr* ("Puppet Theater") in Plovdiv. The hall was filled with a very receptive audience and the emotions were especially evident when the orchestra played the famous song *Dle Yaman*. This song, based on the folk tradition of ancient Armenia, collected and arranged by the famous Armenian priest and musicologist Komitas (or Gomidas in the Western Armenian pronunciation), has become an anthem and a symbol of the Genocide in the diaspora, and one of the most effective means of remembering the tragic past. It is closely linked to the sad fate of Komitas/Gomidas, who fell victim to the Turkish persecutions. Although he survived physically, he suffered from severe psychiatric problems for the rest of his life. The children of the Malvina Manoukyan theater school, supported by the AGBU branch in Plovdiv, rehearsed their roles in the theater version of *The Book of Whispers* for months. In the process, the children were familiarized with the horror of the Genocide. They internalized it so much that they performed impeccably in front of their audience. The eager participation of young Armenians in this commemoration of the traumatic events of the past proves that the descendants of the Genocide survivors are experiencing a form of "postmemory," associated with an "obligation that was placed upon them to be the bearers of hopes and aspirations of a whole people" (Boyajian & Grigorian 1986: 13). The narrative of the Genocide and the struggle for its recognition is being transmitted directly not only to a new generation but also to an external audience whose approbation is required to legitimize the new generation's efforts at remembrance.[37]

---

37 From their side, the Armenians have expressed their gratitude to their adoptive country in a variety of ways in the course of the last century. One example is a short video released in 2018 in various media, in which the Bulgarian Armenians

5.4. Written Culture and Genocide Remembrance in the *Parekordzagani Tzain*

As part of the numerous initiatives to commemorate the events of 1915–1918, a contest was announced on the pages of *Parekordzagani Tzain* in early 2015. The aim was to award a text (a piece of prose, an essay, a poem, or a dramaturgical work) written on the theme of the 100th anniversary of the Genocide. Several poems were published in issue 152 of the newspaper. They were all in Bulgarian and written by Plovdiv citizens (probably all of Armenian origin, although we cannot say for sure) as well as by authors from other Bulgarian cities. Among them is a very poignant poem written by a 14-year-old girl of Armenian descent from Plovdiv named Vartuhi Erdeklyan. The title of the composition is *Pomnja* ("I remember" in Bulgarian):

> And how many Armenians were not born?
> Wanderers tossed away in foreign worlds
> Starting over from scratch, on their way they marched
> creating our forefathers, up to what we are now.

> Today – now we are here
> The resettlers from the genocide survivors
> One to the East, the other to the West
> The heirs of those who chose to live.

> Nobody dies after their death
> As long as the memory remains with the living ones
> As long as someone wakes up with their name
> And goes to sleep with a smile for their deeds.

> From my eyes tears flow...
> Tears of joy they are
> For I know who my ancestors were
> And I remember ... So do you remember too?

---

turned to their "adoptive" Balkan country, declaring profound gratitude for its hospitality and solidarity.

This poem clearly shows the intergenerational transmission of trauma, the creative power of "postmemory" in later generations, and the importance of the affiliative actions of institutions aimed at the re-individualization of cultural memory (Hirsch 2008: 115). A 14-year-old girl is probably no less than a great-grandchild of a Genocide survivor, but that does not mean that her experience of postmemory is any less intense than that of the generations before her. Her composition is also proof that while Armenians around the world are divided in many ways, they are united by one thing: the goal of keeping alive the memory of the catastrophe that traumatized their ancestors (Gaunt 2014: 10).

The fact that this text, along with many others, was published in the pages of *Parekordzagani Tzain* also proves the extent to which personal memory passed down privately through generations can be transformed into a form of cultural memory (Assman 2008) producing meaning for the entire collectivity. Indeed, Armenians use their institutional channels to create images, monuments, and other forms of commemoration that express the communal, shared identity of the Diaspora. I believe that in the experiences of remembering the Genocide, the line between individual and collective suffering is extremely fluid.

In 2015, more and more articles were published in the *Parekordzagani Tzain* that dealt with the memories and personal stories of the descendants of Genocide survivors. An example of this is a text published in issue 151 of the newspaper titled "Memories of Hayganush: A story about the fate of my parents during the Armenian Genocide (1915–1922)", written by Mrs. Hayganush Djezarlyan. In her article, the author recalls her parents' life in the city of Van, their daily activities, and contacts with other communities such as Kurds and Turks before the Genocide. She then recounts the horrific experiences lived by her mother and father before they were able to settle and find refuge in the Bulgarian city of Varna. The story is written clearly and quite essentialistically, but as a personal narrative it still has the power to engage the reader in a touching, emotional family history: the connection to the broader history and destiny of the Armenian nation allows it to channel a stream of empathy and participation. All Armenians can identify with such tragic narratives. When they are published, the sense of community is affirmed and strengthened. This feeling becomes a valuable tool to soothe the wounds and traumas of the intergenerational experience of the Genocide. At the same time, these testimonies recall the vanished traces of a lost homeland: the territory and cultural coordinates of the historical lands of Western Armenia, in which the city of Van on the shores of Lake Van (in today's Southeastern Turkey) occupied a special place.

The commemoration of the 100th anniversary of the Genocide was also an opportunity to strengthen the ties of the Plovdiv community with the initiatives of other diasporic communities. The inter-diasporic links are maintained and made visible through a dense network of cooperation. A significant initiative at the European level in 2015 was the Armenian Worldwide Reading, which took place in several cities on April 21. The reading was organized by the International Literature Festival in Berlin to raise awareness among a European audience about a topic that is still alive and hotly debated. In Plovdiv, the reading took place at the Ethnographic Museum. The program included excerpts from novels by Romanian-Armenian, Soviet-Armenian, and Bulgarian-Armenian authors, respectively, Varujan Vosganian, Kachik Dashtents, and Suren Vetsigian.

5.5. The Turkish Factor in the Armenian-Bulgarian Context

With its links to diasporic structures and through its own initiatives, the AGBU branch in Plovdiv has always been an important actor, combining the local Armenian dimension with a transnational one. An important aspect that should be highlighted is that it also focuses on events and developments in Turkey and cooperates with groups such as the Hrant Dink Foundation and the DurDe Platform. The Turkish element is unavoidable, as Turkey, the neighboring country, is the ultimate destination for all news related to the struggle for Genocide recognition. In issue 151 of *Parekordzagani Tzain*, published in April 2015, the front page of the newspaper has a black background with the following words, in English: "Recognize the Armenian Genocide. 24 April 2015." A Turkish flag appears within the "o" of "Recognize." In the weeks leading up to and following the 100th anniversary, the *Parekordzagani Tzain* paid particular attention to the way the anniversary was commemorated in Istanbul. For example, a delegation from AGBU Europe (which is headquartered in Brussels) participated in a ceremony in Istanbul, along with the anti-racist movement EGAM and many other organizations. AGBU encouraged young Armenians from all over the world to join other members of the diaspora in this city to share the important commemoration day with the city's residents.[38] I was among them. In Turkey's largest city, a large demonstration procession moved from Istiklal Caddesi to Taksim Square. Early in the morning, an event was held in front of the old Haydarpaşa railroad station on the Asian side of the city, from which the first trains carrying Armenian intellectuals to Anatolia departed in 1915. Indeed, this was a defining moment that helped solidify diaspora ties and carry demands for justice across a variety of transnational contexts.

As far as the Turkish factor is concerned, in the pages of *Parekordzagani Tzain*, a very special place is dedicated to the memory of Hrant Dink, editor-in-chief and one of the founders of the important bilingual Turkish-Armenian publication *Agos* Weekly, who was assassinated outside the newspaper's Istanbul office on January 19, 2007. Dink was an important figure in the struggle for recognition of the historical truth of the Genocide. In the diaspora, his memory is associated with a "new Armenian martyrdom" and has become a symbol of the ongoing injustice against ethnolinguistic minorities in Turkey. Since his death, a strong need has been felt among Bulgarian Armenians to make his reportages, and his struggle for the recognition of the genocide by the Turkish government known to a wide Armenian and Bulgarian audience. "Nobody knows what his reports were about, why he wrote them, what his thoughts and positions were, nobody knows his civic conscience, and that is why we want this to reach not only Armenians but Bulgarians as well" (Personal interview with Hripsime Erniasyan, October 2010).

The staff of the AGBU Plovdiv worked hard on the Bulgarian translation of his writings. As a result, the book *Two Close Peoples, Two Distant Neighbours. Armenia – Turkey* (in Bulgarian: *Dva blizki Naroda*, dva dalečni săseda. Armenija – Turcija) was published in 2011, a work that presents a selection of Hrant Dink's articles published in *Agos*.

---

38 See "1915–2015: Turks, Armenians, Europeans: Let's Commemorate the Armenian Genocide Together in Turkey," https://www.remember24april1915.eu/

This has helped to make Dink's work known to a wider Bulgarian population. A second volume of the Turkish-Armenian journalist's writings is to be published soon. The AGBU's publishing activity fits into the context of initiatives to commemorate not only the journalist's death but also the Armenian Genocide, a question that moves the entire community and to which the Bulgarian public adheres significantly.

In a sense, Armenians and Bulgarians are allies, both in dealing with the Ottoman past of subjugation and in their thorny relationship with today's Turkey. The attitude of Bulgarian Armenians toward Turkey is complex and somewhat contradictory. Some Armenians in Plovdiv can still speak the Turkish language, which was passed down to them by the generation that survived the Genocide (Miceva 2001: 153). If we look beneath the surface of suffering and prejudice, we very often find a living heritage of elements of Turkish culture that in some respects (in food, music, etc.) resemble those of the Armenian diaspora itself. However, Armenians are not willing to say too much (or talk too openly) about their relationship with the Turkish world and a shared cultural past. The psyche of the nation in the diaspora is still dominated by a sense of threat. As long as the issue of Genocide recognition remains unresolved, Armenian mistrust of Turks will be passed on to future generations and reaffirmed in many ways. Since much of the Armenian diaspora in Plovdiv is descended from Genocide survivors, all members of the community are still personally affected by the horrors that took place in the Ottoman Empire in the early 20th century. Almost everyone has a personal family story to tell that is connected to the tragic events. The Genocide is the experience that unites all Armenians, and commemorating it is a way to manifest the miracle of the nation's survival despite its dispersion around the world and the ultimate loss of its ancestral homeland. As it was written on the occasion of the 70th anniversary of the Genocide: "[B]y a continued denial by the Turks of the genocide and by the general lack of knowledge and acceptance of the truth... the psychological genocide continues. As a consequence, generations of

Armenians are unwilling and unable to put aside the events of 1915 as past history" (Boyajian & Gregorian 1986: 183).[39]

---

[39] Parts of this chapter have been previously published in the article, "The role of the newspaper Parekordzagani Tzain and its related institutions in the preservation of language and identity in the Armenian community of Plovdiv," which appeared in the Bulletin of Transilvania University of Braşov. Series IV—Philology. Cultural Studies, Vol. 11 (60), no. 1, 2018, and in the article "Preserving the Postmemory of the Genocide: The Armenian Diaspora's Institutions in Plovdiv," which appeared in Acta Universitatis Carolinae—Studia Territorialia 2, 2018. I thank the editors of the Bulletin of the Transilvania University of Braşov. Series IV—Philology. Cultural Studies and of Studia Territorialia for their permission to reproduce excerpts from the articles in this book.

6. The Genocide and the Lost Homeland in the Local Literature

Abstract: This chapter focuses on a series of examples of written production of the Armenian community in Plovdiv, illustrating the different publications of the publishing houses Armen Tur and Parekordzagan. Particular attention is devoted to Suren Vetsigian's book *Autobiography, His Guiding Hand to Serve My People*, a memoir on the Armenian Genocide. Finally, I briefly analyze the cookbook with the Armenian diaspora and explain its value in terms of cultural memory preservation.

Keywords: Armenian written production, local Armenian books, Suren Vetsigian, genocide memoir, Armenian recipes cookbook

6.1. Cultural Survival and the Significance of the Written Language

Among the Armenian diaspora in Plovdiv, as discussed in the previous chapters, much is being done to support the endangered Western Armenian language by promoting literacy. There are good practical reasons for this, the most obvious of which is the need to effectively convey community-relevant information (in this case, the memory of the genocide, cultural elements, and distinctive symbols of Armenian identity) in this language, which undoubtedly requires some form of writing. But the reasons for this insistence on literacy run even deeper, involving elements of a clearly defined ideological nature. In many societies, beliefs prevail that decisively favor the written form of language over the oral. As can be seen from the situations described so far, Armenian culture offers a particularly clear example of this. Therefore, it is useful to pay close attention not only to the actual practices of acquiring writing and reading skills in the language but also to the dominant ideologies about literacy in the society. And these, significantly, like a snake biting its own tail, spread largely through writing itself.

In this context, it is important to note that the extent to which the majority of the population has the ability to read and write is not necessarily the only relevant fact regarding the state of literacy practices in the

Armenian language. Indeed, if literacy is viewed as a social practice rather than a mere technology, it has the potential to affect society in a general way and can have a significant impact even on those who have not mastered its techniques (Field 2001: 106). In other words, one should not equate the written word and its power with the literate community because the two groups do not coincide. When literacy generates relations valid for the entire community, both the illiterate and the literate can participate in its practices. Thus, the depth of their penetration of the social environment should not be confused with the spread of literacy in the traditional sense. Building an ideology of literacy that allows large numbers of people to identify with, and even marginally participate in, the collective practices of signification of writing may be much more important to the maintenance of language than the spread of actual literacy. In this regard, the Armenian press in Plovdiv plays a key role, as it is able to spread positive ideologies regarding the Armenian script among members of the community of different ages and social backgrounds, even if this is done mainly through the use of the Bulgarian language. The general sense that important things can be accomplished by writing in an endangered language is fundamental in this context. And so, attempts to raise the prestige of the written language, reflected in acts of acceptance and recognition even from outside the community, can make one of the strongest contributions to the ideology of language preservation. The Armenians of Plovdiv are successful in this regard because of their distinctiveness of being a transnational community that maintains important relations with other Armenians in Bulgaria, with Armenians from other countries, and with Armenians from the Republic of Armenia through various initiatives carried out by their associations.

According to Petrucci's definition, "well-read people," are those who "master without difficulty, both in terms of text production and text use, all the graphic types in use in the societies to which they belong; moreover, they can generally compose texts in one or more languages other than their mother tongue" (Petrucci 2007: 20, my translation). In the case of the Armenians of Plovdiv, and in relation to the Armenian language, this group of people definitely represents a minority, and it is mainly constituted by those who work in the field of culture, such as journalists, teachers, writers, and churchmen. When considering the reference category in which writing circulates, it is necessary to keep in mind that it differs from the community of speakers, in the sense that there is no complete correspondence between the two. Writers may be a single person, a small group, or a social class, but they are certainly less numerous than the speakers. Instead, there are people who enjoy only the writing produced by others, who are only readers (Cardona 2009: 66). Since graphic production, even more than verbal production, is characterized by the fact that it can be socially controlled, writing proves to be a strong instrument of power. Educated people can also exercise influence over a community's self-perception, its national self-identification, and its constituent symbols (Smith 2009: 31). In the Armenian context, as we have already seen, one of the most powerful symbols is precisely the alphabet. Writing is the prerogative of certain strata and social classes, but by virtue of the prestige it enjoys even among those who do not possess it, the ideologies which accompany it radiate into wider circles (Cardona 2009: 154).

In this context, the written production of the Armenian community in Plovdiv can be considered as a promotion of Armenian culture and memory, although it is published mainly in Bulgarian. This seemingly contradictory fact can be explained by considering the use of important symbols such as the Armenian martyr, the Armenian alphabet, and the lost homeland (including Mount Ararat) as particularly recurring themes in the community's written production, as elements that support specific ideologies about Armenian identity. In this way, Mesrop Mashtot, the alphabet, his translation activity, the old manuscripts, etc. are revived and re-signified in their present value as symbols of the evolving history of Armenian written culture, which continues to create meaning even in the micro-context of a diaspora community such as that of Armenians in Plovdiv.

6.2. The Books Published by the *Armen Tur* and the *Parekordzagan*/AGBU

Since the late 1990s, thanks to the *Parekordzagan*/AGBU Organization, the promotion of literature in this city was activated through cooperation with the local publishing house *Armen Tur*. This was the first publishing house of translated Armenian literature in Plovdiv, and *Parekordzagan* provided part of the funding for some of these activities. Books were published that were either translated from Armenian or written by Armenian authors in Bulgaria. These included poetry, novels, autobiographies, history, etc. Today, the *Armen Tur* Publishing House no longer exists (it ceased its activities sometime after 2008–2009), while the AGBU/*Parekordzagan* has established its own publishing house with the same name. In this context, the role of translators is crucial, as the published works are almost exclusively in Bulgarian in order to reach all segments of society. The most important Armenian-Bulgarian translator for many years until his death in 2016 was Mr. Agop Ormandjyan, Professor of Armenian Studies at the University Sveti Kliment Ohridski in Sofia.

Among the many works that Ormandjyan contributed to the realization, his *Imennik* "Glossary" containing Armenian first names in Cyrillic and Armenian script is an interesting case. This work was conceived as a tool to help the reader to pronounce and write Armenian personal names correctly. The motivation for writing this book was based on the "unbelievable and unpleasant distortions and transformations of Armenian names transcribed and transliterated in Cyrillic and Latin letters, not to mention their spelling in the electronic media and in personal contacts" (Ormandjyan 2000: 4). A distinctive feature of the glossary is that the names are first transcribed and transliterated in Cyrillic and then in the Armenian alphabet. This book contains about 1,800 personal names of Armenian origin used in the Armenian diaspora worldwide as well as in the Republic of Armenia. It is intended to satisfy the interest of Armenians and Bulgarians and to prevent errors in spelling in Cyrillic script in the media and in official documents, as well as mispronunciation of these names in the media and at public events.

Other published books include the 1997 Bulgarian translation of Hovhannes Tumanyan's work *The Daredevils of Sassoun* (after its main hero David of Sassoun - in Armenian), one of the most important Armenian national epics. It dates back to the 8th century and describes the deeds of the hero David, who succeeds in driving the Arabs out of Armenia. Among the other titles we find the 1999 book by Mihran Bohosyan *And Noah descended from Ararat: Armenian Myths, Legends and Sagas*, and the 2012 book by Vardan Balyan, *Zagadkata Zangezur* ("The Mystery of Zangezur") about the archeological site of Zorats Karer in Southern Armenia. Recently, in 2021, a book about Garegin Ter-Harutyunyan (better known by his guerrilla name "Karekin Nzhdeh") entitled *General Karekin, a Hero of Two Nations* was published, dealing with the life of this important figure who participated in the struggles against the Ottoman Empire in the Caucasus and in the Balkans (Salbashyan 2021).

Last but not least, among the books published by *Armen Tur* and *Parekordzagan* in the last 25 years are important literary works related to the Genocide, such as a novel *The Call of Plowmen* by the Soviet-Armenian writer Khachik Dashtents (1910–1974), issued in 2003 in the Bulgarian translation by Agop Ormandjyan under the title *Zovăt na oračite*.

This important work of 20th-century Armenian literature, set at the turn of the 19th century, deals with the events experienced by a young Armenian in the Anatolian territories under Ottoman rule. The protagonist takes up arms and joins the revolutionary partisan movement of the Armenian Fedayi, who fight for liberation from the Turkish yoke and stage two uprisings against the Ottoman authorities and Kurdish tribes in 1894 and 1904. The heroes of the liberation are peasants, ordinary people forced to defend their rights. This book is particularly relevant to the Bulgarian context. Indeed, in it the young protagonist recounts episodes from his own life in the form of short individual stories in which legendary names from the national liberation movement are mentioned, such as Antranik,[40] a famous fighter who is still very much alive in the memory of Bulgarian Armenians, mainly because he fought for the Bulgarians during the Balkan wars. Dashtents, a native of Sason in southeastern Turkey, was a survivor of the Genocide and spent the rest of his life in Soviet Armenia.

As part of the initiatives for the 100th anniversary of the Armenian Genocide, the Bulgarian translation of the novel *Among the Ruins (Sred Razvalinite)* by Zabel Yesayan was published. The work describes the massacres of Armenians in the Anatolian city of Adana in 1909, which the author herself witnessed. It documents the destructiveness of the pogroms, which were directed against the defenseless Armenian population and were a prelude to the Genocide of the Young Turks. Yesayan was herself persecuted and was the only woman among the Armenian intellectuals deported from Istanbul to Anatolia on April 24, 1915, at the beginning

---

40 Andranik in Eastern Armenian.

of the Genocide. She escaped and fled first to Bulgaria and then to the Caucasus, where she worked with other refugees who had survived the massacres. She continued to document the aftermath of the persecution against the Armenians. Another initiative in 2015 was the translation into English of the book by Suren Vetsigian (1905–1961), *Voden ot Boga v služba na naroda si* (In its English version: *Autobiography. His Guiding Hand to Serve My People*), which had already been published in 2001 by the *Armen Tur* in Plovdiv. This book, a memoir on the Genocide written by a very important personality of the Armenian diaspora in Plovdiv, will now be examined in more detail.

6.3. Suren Vetsigian's Genocide Memoir

Handwritten in English in 1947–1948, the book *Autobiography. His Guiding Hand to Serve My People* was translated into Bulgarian by the author's son Horen in the late 1990s and published in Plovdiv in 2001 with limited circulation. Fourteen years after its first appearance, the AGBU/ Parekordzagan issued the English version of the book in a digital format. This publication initiative was related to the commemorations of the centenary of the Armenian Genocide of 1915 and the 110th anniversary of Vetsigian's birth. The main motivation was AGBU's desire for the book to reach a wider audience and give visibility to an important work that has not yet received the attention it deserves. Vetsigian's narrative focuses on the Genocide of one and a half million unarmed Armenians, which he reconstructs from the perspective of common Armenian destiny and history as well as from his personal life. He describes life in his hometown of Shabin Karahisar before World War I, the vicissitudes he faced as a displaced and orphaned child, and the migration experiences as a young man who moved to Greece, Bulgaria, the United States, and finally to the city of Plovdiv to follow his calling to serve his people, that is, the local Armenian community. Vetsigian became a prominent member of the Armenian minority in Plovdiv, as he was the director of the Armenian school, journalist, and writer. In addition, he used his experiences as a Genocide survivor to further his mission and maintain a sense of Armenianness among members of the diaspora.

The book, which contains an analysis and commentary on events, often based on written sources,[41] extends to 1948 when the author's position as the director of the Armenian School in Plovdiv is putting him through a difficult period in the early years of the communist regime. In the preface to his autobiography, Vetsigian explains that his decision to write it was motivated primarily by the hope that it would help shed light on the history of an "unfortunate nation" (Vetsigian 2014: 4). His goal was to help inform about the historical truth of the tragic events experienced by the Armenian people in the last years of the Ottoman Empire and to provide a response to the books written by the Turks that painted a distorted picture of historical events. The memoir of Suren Vetsigian is among the direct testimonies of survivors that remained unpublished for a long time.[42]

Vetsigian was born in 1905 in Shabin Karahisar, a village in northeastern Anatolia, in the actual Giresun Province. He was still a boy when the massacres took place in his hometown and withstood the adverse circumstances with extraordinary strength. It may be noted that in the context of commemorating the Genocide, Vetsigian expresses a particular point of view that is largely shared by the AGBU in Plovdiv: while mourning the victims of such terrible events, one should not forget the bravery of those who organized active resistance, as in the case of the Armenian uprising in the town of Shabin Karahisar (Payaslian 2004), in which he personally participated and which he describes in his autobiography. These events became historically known, since the revolts lasted for almost the entire month of June 1915.[43] Vetsigian enriches his account of the tragic events with historical facts that make the Armenians appear not only as victims but also as fighters: his hometown acquired a special value for his later intellectual activity as a paradigm of civic resistance, which can be inferred from a later mention of his largest unpublished work, *History of Shabin Karahisar*. The other element is the importance of the native language and written culture for the Armenians living in the Anatolian territories. In the first section of the book, which deals with his native

---

41 Among the quoted ones, Lepsius, 1919; Palakian 1922; Barby, 1917.
42 See: Der-Garabedian 2004, Hamamdjian 2004, Minassian 2020.
43 The uprisings of Shabin Karahisar have been narrated by author Aram Haigaz, who survived the siege and the following deportation. See: Haigaz 1935.

region, the author repeatedly emphasizes that the Armenians living there, unlike the Kurds and Turks, were a literate nation.

> In the short period from 1908 to 1915, when the conditions allowed it, Armenians made such cultural progress that they made the Turks green with envy. They opened cultural clubs, books were published. In the entire Ottoman Empire, the number of students in 1915 was 242 thousand, and the small Armenian population alone had 120 thousand students. (Vetsigian 2014: 34)

The motif of his hometown's heroic resistance, in conjunction with his relationship to his mother tongue, became the most important component of his external and internal path of salvation and the crucial element on which his later identity was based. After losing his parents due to the tragic events in his hometown, Vetsigian was enslaved for months by Turkish families in various villages, lost his Christian identity and language, and adopted the Muslim name of "Husein." Later, thanks to meeting a Greek refugee of the same age, he managed to escape to the city of Sivas. At some point, after having spent some time in Sivas, Vetsigian was taken to the nearby Surp (Saint) Nshan Monastery, a famous 11th-century site of special significance to Armenians as it preserved a throne, crown, and other valuable items that had belonged to the kings of the ancient Armenian Artsruni dynasty. The author mentions the regret felt when he learned that the treasures had been looted by the governor of Sivas, the monastery plundered, and all the valuable crosses, icons, and kilims stolen. This was indeed one of the countless examples of the destruction of Armenian cultural heritage[44] that took place during the years of the Genocide (Ferrari 2019: 20).

The author countered the despair with the power of the Armenian language, which he rediscovered while being housed in this monastery. He heard some of the young nuns speak it among themselves: "I would listen to their conversation in Armenian and understand all, but I did not reveal my nationality" (Vetsigian 2014: 67). Vetsigian experienced this moment as a kind of second rebirth. All this happened in the winter of 1919, after

---

44 See more on such examples (which include churches and other buildings, family archives, khachkar) in Adalian 2013: 133.

the signing of the armistice: as Vetsigian soon found out, he was in an or-phanage run by the Armenian Near East Aid.

> The one thing, for which I will always be grateful in the orphanage life is that very soon began the teaching of reading and writing. When classification was made, I was among the best. (...) I loved books. For hours I would read. My teachers had to remind me that I should play a little. The library of the college was at our disposal. I eagerly read many Armenian books and the number of the not yet read was getting smaller. I began to worry a little. (Vetsigian 2014: 105)

The love and devotion for the mother tongue keep growing until they turn into a passion for reading and writing. In this way, Vetsigian seems to sub-limate the loss of his family and hometown and find an inner dimension of belonging. Despite such progress, the restoration of the connection with the native language remained a problem. The author repeatedly expresses regret toward his fellow Armenians who did not know their language at all, or not well enough, or refused to use it. He also describes how religion was not taught to the children in a rational and esthetic way:

> The translation of the Bible in modern Armenian, done by missionaries, had been done badly. Its style has none of the beauty possessed by the ancient translation. [...] [Some of t]he speakers in church or chapel exercises [...] didn't know enough Armenian [...]. Even though a child, I was very critical toward all speakers. Especially mistakes of style or language used to annoy me. (Vetsigian 2014: 74)

As a student of Anatolia College in Greece,[45] an American institution, he earned the respect of his Armenian teachers because of his matchless language. He had learned a great deal about Armenian history and memo-rized long poems, which he proudly recited at public events. He wrote "se-rious and nice compositions which occasionally would call public praise" (Vetsigian 2014: 91). In his circle of friends, he advocated using pure Arme-nian "with no mixture of Turkish or English words" (Vetsigian 2014: 91). Later, as a student at the School of Religion in Athens, he was disappointed and annoyed to find out that Armenian students spoke mainly in Turkish or preferred to focus only on English. His love for the mother tongue gradually turned into a passion for writing, in addition to reading, and the first newspaper published at the college is an Armenian one, handwritten,

---

45 He arrived in Greece with a ship from the Black Sea city of Samsun, Turkey.

thanks to his initiative. His articles became very popular among the Armenian students. In the refugee camps he visited in Athens, which housed many Armenians who had fled the Genocide (Hassiotis 2002: 100), they all spoke Turkish instead of their mother tongue, which he found "repulsive": "How they did not have enough national pride or self-respect to discard the language of people, who had inflicted so much suffering on them? That was beyond my comprehension" (Vetsigian 2014: 95).

When Vetsigian moved to the United States to study at Yale, his main regret was not meeting Armenians who spoke Armenian. Thus, he wrote in his diary:

> O, God, there isn't a single Armenian with whom I might exchange a few words in Armenian. How I long for an Armenian. Sometimes I read my Gospels in the classic Armenian, but that is not enough. I must talk with myself, no other way. Sometimes it seems to me, that I shall forget the language before I leave this country. What a melting pot this country is! Whoever falls in it loses his identity within a short time. There are nominally Armenians who either don't know Armenian, or don't want to use it. Only once I saw two young women talking Armenian. How happy I was to hear them talk! If they were not young women, I would go to talk to them. (Vetsigian 2014: 143)

The experience of being an Armenian in the United States proved ambivalent for the author. On the one hand, he adapted quite well to the context without giving up his Armenian identity, and even reinforced his sense of being Armenian through contact with yet another foreign context. On the other hand, he found that this was not the case with other Armenians living in the country, as he felt there was a high pressure to assimilate.[46] This threat of assimilation, in his view, nullified any prospect of remaining in the country to preserve Armenian identity in the local diaspora. Based on this realization, he figured out that his place was closer to the people he could help, in a sociocultural environment that preserved some of the characteristics of his Anatolian hometown in terms of "Oriental" (Vetsigian 2014: 104) coexistence of religions, ethnicities, and cultures. Therefore,

---

46 He writes about this risk: "What a melting pot this country is! Whoever falls in it loses his identity within a short time" (Vetsigian 2014: 100). And then: "Armenians in the USA do not need me – already individual nations have no chance to perpetuate their existence there" (Vetsigian 2014: 129).

after graduating from the Divinity School at Yale, the author renounced the opportunity to enroll in a doctoral program and settled in the Bulgarian city of Plovdiv. Here, Vetsigian became a prominent member of the Armenian community and director of the Armenian School in Plovdiv, a position he held for a good 15 years, not without difficulties. Besides, he also pursued his vocation as a writer, publishing numerous articles in the various Armenian newspapers active before the beginning of the communist rule, among which the *Balkanyan Mamul* and *Paros*, on various subjects: religious, political, historical, pedagogical. From 1934 to 1946, he wrote a total of 181 articles, until these newspapers were closed by the new regime.

In addition to articles, Vetsigian also wrote a number of books, some of which have been published, others not. Some are textbooks for the Armenian school: on Armenian literature, religion, Armenian history, and Armenian grammar. Others works he wrote are *History of the Armenian School of Plovdiv*, *History of Armenian Literature*, *The Cause of the Armenian Tragedy*, and a historical play, based on the uprisings in his hometown. Unfortunately, he regrets that he could not publish what he considered his most important book, the history of his hometown Shabin Karahisar. In his diary, he formulated the reason for writing this work:

> It is human to sympathize with suffering. We get interested in a wounded animal, in a fallen little bird. Even more we sympathize with human suffering. When that suffering is born with great patience, our sympathy grows greater. But when it is born bravely, heroically, then we are moved to immortalize it in some way. That human sympathy is the cause that moved me to write the history of Shabin Karahisar. I have tried to immortalize the heroism of a few thousands humble folk, who suffered immensely, but heroically and bravely. (Vetsigian 2014: 120)

As a member of the Fellowship of Reconciliation in the United States, an interfaith organization promoting the ideals of justice and nonviolence, he always spoke out against the use of violence and defended values such as brotherhood and peace. Vetsigian's stance against any form of chauvinism also earned him no small amount of trouble among Armenians in Plovdiv. He unfortunately became a kind of outsider, because no social, political, or intellectual niche accommodated the complexity of his views. In January 1949, Vetsigian lost his job as school director (p. 134), and soon after he was deprived of any freedom to speak and write publicly (p. 128). After being jobless for some time, he took a new job as a construction worker. He then was employed as a warehouse supervisor in a woodwork factory in Plovdiv for the rest of his life (p. 2). In Plovdiv, Vetsigian managed to find "his own diaspora" among the many possible ones in the world, that is, a definitive sublimation of his lost homeland through a spiritual and emotional connection with a community of people accepting what Robin Cohen defines as "an inescapable link with their past migration history and a sense of co-ethnicity with others of a similar background" (Cohen 2008: ix).

> The chief reason for my return was that I could never forget the suffering of my people. I felt my duty to serve the remnants of my nation. Otherwise I couldn't explain why God should have saved my life [...]
> I live for my martyred nation, whose sufferings I have shared. After this I can say "I am the Armenian nation." (Vetsigian 2014: 106)

The life of Vetsigian represents, in a way, the exemplary paradigm of the Armenian experience of "love" for the mother tongue. The author touches upon all the major areas in which language plays a key role: reading, writing, education, religion, and printing, and he praises the mother tongue as a pillar of his people's culture. It is very significant that he eventually became the director of the Tutunjyan Armenian School, and in his autobiography, the author also included letters from the Armenian citizens of Plovdiv expressing their gratitude for his great services to the Armenian people through his articles, books, and lectures. The publication of his book in Plovdiv offers readers the opportunity to see an example of a concrete commitment to Armenian culture that underlies the ideologies expressed by the local intelligentsia: this does not mean that everyone must write Armenian or become a teacher of Armenian, but in a way it is implied that members of the community must be aware of the importance of the Armenian language and share "ethnogenic" ideas about it in order to be truly Armenian. In this sense, the discourse on writing and written culture requires and provokes participation.

What is perhaps most striking in Vetsigian's linguistic situation is the fact that his memoir was not originally written in Armenian. We can surmise that he chose English precisely to reach a wider audience, as many other writers did (see Haroutyunian 2015:43), and since important friends he had in the United States, many of whom were not Armenians, had encouraged him to write. The creation of Armenian literary works in a foreign language was an issue among writers and intellectuals in the diaspora, especially for Genocide survivors (Oshagan 1986: 225). Multilingualism is and has always been a reality for diaspora Armenians (Sahakyan 2018): the languages Vetsigian knew were Armenian, English, Turkish, Bulgarian, and probably some Greek. Turkish always remained only an oral language for him, which he learned while still in his hometown in the Ottoman Empire and which was most likely associated with painful memories and emotions; he never chose to write anything in this language.

6.4. The Cookbook of the Ancestors, a Source of Memory on the Lost Homeland

In the Armenian diaspora experience, memory and language remain the privileged means for introspection: a return to the sacred homeland, a "symbolic journey to the source" (Grace 2007: 13) is impossible, since ancient Armenia, as it was, is lost forever, deprived of its cultural landmarks and most of its inhabitants (see Ferrari 2019: 20 ff). Vetsigian's attachment to the Armenian language since his departure from Anatolia is a key that allows us to interpret his personal history as a continuous search for a form of spirituality in Armenian culture itself. The survival of the "nation" and the preservation of its culture are viewed as political and spiritual ideals for Armenian intellectuals in the diaspora (Peroomian 2003: 171).

While describing the tragic events, Vetsigian's autobiography, similar to other works by Genocide survivors, valorizes the Armenian component in the Ottoman cultural landscape and reconstructs the patterns of existence of a past world that has been completely erased in these territories. Similar to Jewish narratives about their lost homeland in Europe, this literature not only nostalgically preserves the image of past conditions but also brings them into the present and "gives them cultural significance well beyond that of historically concrete sites" (Zarecka 1994: 92). As a result, we can observe that "myths emerge almost naturally here, as the sense of loss acquires permanence" (Zarecka 1994: 92). In the case of the Armenians in Plovdiv, the AGBU's publication and promotion of these literary works is coupled with a desire to transmit the cultural and national memory of the Genocide, in line with its mission to preserve a specific vision of Armenian identity among future generations of Armenians in the diaspora.

Another way to foster a sense of belonging to the lost homeland is through cuisine. Indeed, an important AGBU publication in 2019 was the book *V sveta na armenskata kuhnja* ("In the World of Armenian Cuisine"). I must admit that over the years I have very rarely found Armenians my age or younger who had read any of the books published by the *Parekordzagan* or the *Armen Tur* in Plovdiv. However, this book is definitely an exception because it was on everyone's mouth, and the same editor, Hripsime Erniasyan, told me that it was the most successful book ever published by the AGBU publishing house, even though it was the most expensive (four times more expensive than the others). Cooking is indeed an accessible language that allows people to explore their culture, share its elements in daily life, and learn about the past.

The book is hardback, consists of 300 pages, and presents 500 recipes with 240 color photos illustrating 15 main categories of Armenian cuisine. It is a pleasant introduction to the folklore and traditions of the old generations of Armenians and reconstructs in detail an integral part of the Armenian way of life. The work on this book took five years and was made possible thanks to the enthusiastic responses of Bulgarian Armenians (not only from the city of Plovdiv) to the AGBU announcements and invitations to provide culinary recipes of their parents or ancestors who lived in the lands of Western Armenia. This was an opportunity for respondents to share the memories of their ancestors that they had preserved through the culinary history of their families. The Bulgarian Armenians who contributed to this book come from many cities: Šumen, Plovdiv, Dobrič, Sofia, Jambol, Sliven, Pazardžik, Varna, and Bistritsa. The recipes were handed down from their ancestors who had survived the Genocide and came from cities and towns such as Çorlu (Turkish Thrace), Rodosto, Shabin Karahisar, Malgara (Malkara), Edirne, Kars, Bandırma, and Kayseri. The cook of the most important Armenian restaurant in Plovdiv, "Erevan," also contributed to this volume.

These recipes refer to the typical dishes prepared in the historical lands of "Western Armenia": these are quite different from the ones prepared in the Republic of Armenia, and come from Arapgir (a town in Malatya province), Ağın (town of Elazığ province), Diyarbakır, Maraş (Kahramanmaraş), Zeytun, (Süleymanlı, also known as Zeitun, a city in Kahramanmaraş province), Musa Ler (the area of the famous[47] Musa Dagh mountain, in the Hatay province), Urfa, Muş.

The Armenian cuisine in the territories of Western Armenia was significantly influenced by the contact with a variety of national and ethnic groups and in turn influenced other cultures, as we read in the introduction to this book:

> Invaders and conquerors from all parts of the world passed through the ancient Armenian land, leaving behind memories of dramatic events and taking with them spiritual and material riches. One of them is the culinary mastery of Armenians, reflected in traditional Arabic and Turkish cuisine, and more recently among other peoples of Europe and Asia, including Greeks, Bulgarians, Russians, Georgians and so on. There is no doubt that today's civilization has its origin in the Old Testament's Garden of Eden, which, according to legend and the latest historical information, is located between the lakes of Van, Urmia and Sevan. This blessed land is the home of the wine, the wheat grain and the apricot, but also of the pomegranate, the plum, the fig... The pomegranate seeds are a symbol of Armenians scattered all over the world, and another symbol of Armenia is the apricot, whose Latin name Prunus armeniaca unequivocally indicates its place of origin. (My translation from Bulgarian)

In the first pages of the book, reference is also made to Mount Ararat (in present-day Turkey), where, according to biblical legend, Noah's Ark came to rest. The Ararat is considered one of the strongest symbols of Armenian identity, epitomizing the highest peak in the millenary history of the Armenian people which, as here emphasized, has been a path of salvation, in terms of spiritual values. Symbols feed national pride and represent a revered duty for essentialist notions of identity, along with ancient Armenian structures such as the "sacred" Armenian family, which "nourishes the roots of traditions and keeps the fire of heritage alive" (Erniasyan 2019: 9). The unique atmosphere of the

---

47 See the book *The Forty Days of the Musa Dagh* by Austrian author Franz Werfel, describing the events here during the Armenian Genocide.

Armenian home is indeed unthinkable without the aroma of Armenian cuisine, and this explains the desired role of this publication. The information contained in this book is intended to support the efforts of Bulgarian Armenians to preserve this culinary heritage in the face of new challenges in the global diaspora. The descriptions of the Armenian dishes of the different regions in the lost lands of Western Armenia, now in Turkey, also give us an idea of their way of life and the taste of their varied cuisine in the past.

The recipes in this book are authentic and were passed down orally from grandmothers to grandchildren. These dishes are considered to be a reflection of the original and peaceful Armenian soul; moreover, cooking with these recipes can be considered as an activity that gives daily pleasure and strengthens the connection of the younger generations with the ancestors, folklore, and traditions of elderly Armenians and creates a link to their roots. And for the older generations of Armenians, the recipes in this book can unlock memories of their parents and grandparents and take them back to the traditions and way of life of the past, toward which so many feelings of loss still prevail.

Armenian cuisine is undoubtedly an inseparable part of Armenian identity: it plays a major role in shaping the image, identity, and mindset of a nation. The book *In the World of Armenian Cuisine* serves the purpose of presenting and affirming the complex and rich Armenian national identity to the Bulgarian context, sustaining the preservation of such cultural heritage by exploring and transmitting it, similar to what has been done with other Armenian diasporas in the world. One example of this is the book *Cuisine d'Armenie* published by members of the Armenian diaspora in France in 2017 by Richard and Korin Zarzavatdjian. Since Armenians do not have physical access to their ancestral lands of Western Armenia, that are now part of Turkey, food can help the descendants of genocide survivors imaginatively reach these places by recreating "edible heirlooms" (Dagher-Margosian 2021) in the kitchen. And since Armenian communities are still threatened with assimilation and disappearance in many parts of the world today, every act of Armenian cooking can also be interpreted as a form of resistance (Dagher-Margosian 2021).[48]

---

48 Parts of this chapter have been previously published in the article "Suren M. Vetsigian's lost Armenian homeland and the quest for new spaces of belonging in his *Autobiography. His Guiding and to Serve My People,*" appeared in Studi Slavistici XVIII, 2021. I thank the editors of Studi Slavistici for their permission to reproduce excerpts from this article in this book.

7. The Armenian Linguistic Landscapes of Plovdiv

Abstract: In this chapter, I focus on the identifying function of written language and memory in various spaces that make up the "linguistic landscape" of the city of Plovdiv. I look at examples of public writing such as those appearing on official monuments, on the objects exhibited at the small museum commemorating the victims of the Genocide in the crypt of the Armenian Church, in the inner and outer spaces of the Armenian school, and on the graves at the local Armenian cemetery.

Keywords: public writings, linguistic landscapes of memory, Genocide remembrance, *khachkar*, Armenian graveyard

7.1. The Visual Role of the Armenian Alphabet in Marking the Community's Spaces

The Armenian spaces of the city have an immediate effect on the viewer's field of vision, triggering a kind of approach mechanism. From the reader's point of view, they catch the eye and invite the passerby, the observer (Mc Luhan 1962: 2) whose visual sense has been stimulated, to decipher them.[49] My first visual experience with the Armenian alphabet in Plovdiv took place during an exploratory visit in search of members of this community, when I did not yet know their spaces of representation in the city. Walking through one of the streets surrounding the upper town, I stopped at one point and noticed with great satisfaction an unmistakable sign of their presence: it may seem strange, but this was confirmed to me by a concentrated row of necrologies hanging on a wall and written in Armenian alphabet! What a nice surprise this was, as I had understood that Armenians lived there and that this wall represented an important

---

49 As a matter of fact, every act of writing is capable to produce an effect when read, and this effect is not merely reducible to the transmission of the written message but takes place in the modality in which a certain statement is presented to the reader (Fraenkel 2010: 36).

boundary—the beginning of their "territory" within the city—and that moreover, they wrote in Armenian. In Plovdiv, it is not surprising that all the places of the Armenian community are marked with letters of their alphabet: the effect is certainly immediate and evokes a perceptual reaction of cultural diversity.

So I strolled through the narrow streets of the upper town and finally, after a short time, I found the heart of the community, namely the complex hosting the cultural center, the Armenian Apostolic Church, the Chapel, the bell tower, and school, all surrounded by walls, a dense space in whose courtyard children were playing. I also immediately noticed many examples of public writings in the form of plaques, monuments, painted writings on the walls, etc. Almost all of them were bilingual in Armenian and Bulgarian, but there predominantly Bulgarian, but there were some exceptions with writings in Armenian exclusively. A large area of writing was waiting to be read by me... The former *armenska mahala*, that is, the old Armenian quarter of the city, is the most important place to observe the Armenian linguistic landscape as well as the symbolic practices of collective identity construction in space. Armenians show a special sensitivity and affection for all objects written with their alphabet, and when they have the opportunity, they obviously mark their presence with their language—and thus with their writing system. Although, as we have seen in the previous chapters, only part of the community is able to understand and produce the written form of the Armenian language (since writing and reading practices are quite limited), it would be unthinkable not to use it to delimit community spaces and those of highest symbolic importance. It also follows that the Armenian alphabet is not really "read" in most cases but only looked at, captured by the eye: reading does not always correspond to the phonetic decipherment of the letters but is often a mere visualization of their presence (Ong 1982: 124) through the esthetic form of the alphabetic signs, their positioning in space. Nevertheless, the effect will be just as strong with this visual knowledge, and in any case will bring about a situation of emotional identification and participation, since Armenians will hardly be indifferent to the presence of the signs of their alphabet.

The choice of language and alphabet in the official space of a community reveals much about the sense of identity of those who commissioned the examples of public writing (Beroujon 2010). In this regard, it is important to consider that the context in which the Armenians of Plovdiv operate is that of a Bulgarian city where multilingualism and multiculturalism are particularly present. In light of this, the written space is also a way to symbolically take possession of a place and give it a sign that visibly distinguishes it from the rest of the city. The addressees of Armenian writing in public space are not only the members of this community but also outsiders who look at a space in which the elements of a unique alphabet become evident, thanks to their visual immediacy.

As we have already seen, the Armenian lesson at school, the press, the AGBU Organization, and the books play a key role in fostering a collective imagination through the valorization of the alphabet, other national symbols, and the memory of the Genocide. But the lessons, articles, and book pages could not disseminate such a discourse on Armenian survival so effectively were they not supported by an important visual component, namely the images and objects in which Armenian script becomes present and unfolds its equally high symbolic value. The various surfaces on which the Armenian writing manifests itself (see also Kuciukian 1998: 39) thus become active participants in the construction of the discourse on national identity. The latter is based on a transtemporal and translocal feeling of belonging to an ancient and culturally rich Armenian identity one cannot help but feel deeply proud of.

The cases I will describe in this chapter aim to show the importance of written objects and the inscription of places in the processes of symbolic cultivation of Armenian identity in the diaspora: they are examples of the spatial marking of this culture and serve as "context markers" (Bateson 1972: 290 - 335–337) of the "linguistic landscapes of memory" (Selvelli 2023, in print) that were mostly created during the commemoration of important historical events. These sites of public inscriptions, consisting of monuments, objects, and written surfaces, provide an important framework for conveying messages of collective Armenian identity and are particularly useful for transmitting the "postmemory" (Hirsch 2008) of the Genocide. They thus constitute what I define as the linguistic landscapes of memory, that is, sentiments, attributions, and expressions related to collective historical events experienced by the community and manifested and realized in various forms of linguistic and semiotic signs (Jaworski &

Thurlow 2010) that are localized in the physical landscape and enable the formation of collective memory (Moore 2019).

7.2. The *Khachkar* of Plovdiv as a Site of Remembrance

The significance acquired by written culture for Armenians throughout the world is reflected in the enormous value placed not only on books and manuscripts but also on any monument or work of art that bears its traces and can manifest its presence in history and space.

> The enemies of our people in our time seem to be well aware of this, because the first thing they do after occupying a place is to erase Armenian inscriptions in Armenian monuments there. One could cite several examples of the relatively recent attempts by Azeris, Georgians and Turks to destroy evidence of Armenian identity from historical monuments. (Maksoudian 2006: 129)

This quote refers to an unfortunately widespread practice of destroying evidence of the Armenian presence, especially by invaluably damaging some of its most important historical monuments, as has been done to numerous *khachkars* in Azerbaijan and Nagorno-Karabakh.

The tradition of *khachkars*, literally "stone crosses," is undoubtedly one of the most original manifestations of the customs and religiosity of the Armenian people (Ieni 1986: 261). These are stone slabs or stelae with cross decorations and other ornamental motifs, often engraved with inscriptions with Armenian characters. They are considered as purely Armenian works of art, embodying a distinctive character as valuable as the letters of their alphabet. Such monuments, traditionally made of stone, used to be widespread in all historical areas of Western Armenia, in what is now Turkey. In 2005, on the occasion of the 90th anniversary of the beginning of the Genocide, the Plovdiv branch of the AGBU/Parekordzagan organization erected an important monument to the victims of 1915. In accordance with ancient Armenian tradition, the monument was built in the form of a large wooden *khachkar*, inspired by a similar monument in Paris. The stated aim of erecting a *khachkar* in Plovdiv was to contribute to the struggle for recognition of the Armenian Genocide throughout the world, in the hope that the tragic events of 1915 would leave deep imprints in the public's mind.

The *khachkar* was made in the Holy See of Ejmiatsin in the Republic of Armenia, where the Catholicos, the spiritual leader of the Armenian Church, resides, and then transported to Plovdiv. On April 24, 2005, this wooden cross was consecrated in the heart of the Armenian community in Plovdiv. This monument is perhaps the most conspicuous manifestation of the Armenian presence in the city. The pedestal reads in Bulgarian and Armenian: "In memory of the 1,500,000 Armenians, innocent victims of the first Genocide of the 20th century, planned and carried out by the leaders of the Union and Progress Committee Party of the Turkish government in 1915." On the wall to the left of the monument is a marble plaque engraved with the same phrase in English, a more recent one in French, and a final one in Bulgarian, stating that the construction of the *khachkar* was made possible by donations from members of the Armenian diaspora in Paris and New York, a major donor from Plovdiv, and the entire Armenian community of Plovdiv. The inscription confirms the cohesion of the local community as well as its cooperation with the diaspora abroad in initiatives to preserve the memory of the Genocide.

Examples of public writing in the Armenian diasporic context play a crucial mnemonic function: they remind people who the Armenians are, what their past was, and what they suffered. In addition, Armenians also "inscribe" in the memory space the solidarity they shared with those who stood by them in their darkest moments. In front of the entrance to the Armenian community complex is a bust of the poet Peyo Yavorov, who wrote the famous *Armenci* poetry work (see Chapter 2) in honor of the victims of the first massacres in Ottoman Turkey in the 1890s. The monument to Yavorov welcomes all visitors entering the Armenian space, who can read, in Bulgarian, the following inscription: "From the always brave martyr nation," followed by another on the back "From the grateful Armenians." Another monument in the courtyard of the community proves the historical Bulgarian-Armenian alliance and solidarity and is located not far from the *khachkar*. A sentence in Bulgarian reads: "In memory of the Armenian soldiers who fell for Mother Bulgaria." The names of the fallen in the Balkan wars of 1912–1913, World War I (most of them) and World War II follow, written in Armenian.

Among the other examples of public writings one can find in the inner court of the community complex is the plaque commemorating the visit of the great Armenian composer, ethnomusicologist, musician, and religious man Komitas/Gomidas, who, as we read in both Armenian and Bulgarian, "visited Plovdiv from July 4 to 7, 1914, gave a concert, lectured and participated in the sacred liturgy in this church." Komitas is considered to be probably the greatest classical musician of Armenian origin, and the fact that he visited the city and the Armenians there is still a great source of pride in the memory of the community. The plaque thus commemorates this event, which took place just 1 year before the 1915 Genocide, which he directly witnessed and which he survived physically, but unfortunately not psychologically.[50]

Other important symbols appearing in the Armenian community spaces are the images of cultural landmarks embodying elements of the cultural and natural heritage of Western Armenia located in Turkish territories. These are a series of large pictures in the courtyard of the church,[51] such as the ancient Armenian city of Ani in northeastern Turkey (the "City of 1,001 Churches", as it was known in the past), the church of Aghtamar on the island of the same name in Lake Van in southeastern Turkey, and Mount Ararat, which is visible from the Armenian capital of Yerevan but located in Turkey.

In a sense, the monuments erected in the Armenian quarters of the city of Plovdiv and elsewhere in the world are a necessary counterweight to the disappearance and neglect of cultural monuments in the historical territory of Western Armenia. The lost monuments there embodied the "fragments of an ancient and abruptly interrupted history" (Ferrari 2016c: 332, my translation), since a journey through the ancient Armenian territories in Turkey is inevitably a "journey into the void, into a contested and elusive memory, into the consciousness of tragedy" (Ferrari 2016c: 332, my translation). With no way to return to the ancient territories to reclaim their cultural history, Armenians feel the need to mark public space in their new homelands around the world with monuments dedicated to their own past, symbolically affirming their presence and their survival as a nation to any observer.

---

50 Komitas/Gomidas died in 1935 in a psychiatric hospital in France. He had never recovered from the trauma of having directly witnessed the Genocide.
51 Some of them also appear in the interior walls of the Armenian restaurant Erevan.

Figure 7.1. Memorial Plaque to Honor the Visit of Ethnomusicologist and Religious Figure Komitas in June 1914 [Credits: G.S.].

7.3. The Inner and Outer Spaces of the Armenian School

Already during my first visit to the Tutunjyan Armenian School, I had the opportunity to observe the space and notice that it is the place par excellence where, as I expected, numerous references to the alphabet appear. At the entrance of the building, to the left of the door, there is a large board with the logo of the school, consisting of the first three letters of the Armenian alphabet and the first three of the Bulgarian alphabet against the background of a sun. A meaningful way to express the spirit of brotherhood between the two peoples, on which the Armenian identity of Plovdiv is based.

The presence of Mesrop Mashtots on the exterior of the school building is only the first part of a long series of visual elements that accompany the visitor to this institution. Inside the school, in fact, many images and symbols of the Armenian alphabet appear, especially a huge fresco on the wall near the stairs to the upper floor, where the classrooms are located. Mesrop Mashtots and Catholikos Sahak are depicted here with the tablet of the Armenian alphabet. On the main wall of the Armenian classroom there is a large poster with the title "The Invention of the Armenian Letters" in Armenian, on which several pictures follow each other, the most important of which is that depicting the huge stones shaped with the characters of the Armenian alphabet, located in the Republic of Armenia. The image of the so-called "Alphabet park" in the country of yelling stones,[52] near the town of Aparan, more or less neatly arranged on a dry Caucasian soil, can also be found outside the classroom on the wall of a corridor and in other inner spaces of this building. Another very noticeable symbol that appears on the large poster is the famous and valuable golden alphabet board, kept in the Cathedral of Ejmiatsin.

On the walls hung various other symbolic images, one of the strongest of which is the Armenian flag with coat of arms, bearing a special inscription that reads, "I love you, my mother tongue" in Armenian. This object is very powerful in its communicative effectiveness, as it consists of both the Armenian flag and a sentence in its script, which, moreover, is very clear to those who can decipher it (and in school, all children who learn Armenian are able to do so, since it is a very simple sentence and it is addressed mainly to them). This flag bearing the sentence in Armenian arouses deep feelings and thus intense participation in the emotional discourse about the Armenian language, which, however, is not technically the mother tongue for most children at all, since, as mentioned in the first chapter, only a few still speak it at home. Nevertheless, this does not change the fact that ideally it remains the "mother tongue" for all children

---

52 Reference to Osip Mandel'stam's poetry work, *Journey to Armenia*, in which he defines this as the "country of yelling stones".

of Armenian descent, just as the Armenian territories (both the historical ones and the Republic of Armenia) are the "motherland" for Armenians today and in the past.

Just as Mesrop Mashtots is described in the school lessons to children as someone who invented the alphabet "with love," a similar attachment to language is perpetuated and fostered through the messages that appear in various forms in Armenian public spaces which help create and sustain common bonds and a sense of national identity. During the significant celebrations of the school's 175th anniversary in 2009, an "esthetic" policy was adopted in which members of the community were encouraged to model and affirm national symbols in modern ways. Although the intellectual elite is the one responsible for endowing the nation with a distinctive character and a concrete form, the popularity of the images depends in part on the extent to which they reflect and incorporate the values, traditions, and emotions, highlighting the nation's distinctiveness. In 2009, one of the results of this moment of celebration was the design of a plate with the Armenian alphabet tablet, which can be seen hanging not only in private houses but also on the walls of internal public places, such as the editorial office of the newspaper *Parekordzagan Tzain* and the Armenian restaurant Erevan. The alphabet was thus publicly "reified" in the form of a plate that was obviously not intended for eating but for purely decorative purposes. This object embodies the desire of local Armenian actors to have the community gathered around a cultural symbol evoking feelings of respect and reverence. A clear symbolic register is expressed in the choice of the golden letters, conveying the message that these are destined to last in the future and anchor themselves in space and time. Furthermore, these characters constitute a clear reference to the prestigious Armenian writing tradition, alluding to the precious golden alphabet tablet enshrined in Ejmiatsin.

On the occasion of another important anniversary, namely the centenary of the Genocide in 2015, a new inscription element was placed on the wall that borders the schoolyard. It was painted with the following words in Bulgarian and Armenian: "100 years since the Armenian Genocide," and only in Bulgarian: "I remember, I condemn," with two forget-me-not flowers on the side. As mentioned in Chapter 5, on the occasion of the 100th anniversary of the Armenian Genocide, the AGBU branch in Plovdiv promoted the display of the forget-me-not flower, a symbol chosen by the diaspora worldwide to commemorate the terrible events of 1915–1918. The positioning of the forget-me-not on the wall in front of the Armenia School can be interpreted as yet another confirmation of the fact that the existence of the Armenian diaspora ontologically depends on the memory of its past, of its cultural symbols, and the memory of the sufferings and tragedies of its ancestors, which must be transmitted to the youngest generations.

Figure 7.2. Tombstones at the Local Armenian Graveyard [Credits: G.S.].

7.4. The Objects on Display in the Crypt of the Armenian Church

In 2001, on the occasion of the 1700th anniversary of the adoption of Christianity as the state religion in 301 in Armenia, a small exhibition was inaugurated in the crypt of the Armenian Church Surp Kevork. This was made possible, thanks to the voluntary participation of community members who donated their family items in the interest of preserving the collective memory of the pre-Genocide life in the Ottoman Empire. In fact, valuable relics are kept here: the Armenians who settled in the city escaping the terrible persecutions of 1915–1918 brought with them some valuable objects that they had saved from desecration from their churches in Rodosto, Malgara, Çorlu, and Edirne. In a long message published in the newspaper *Parekordzagani Tzain*, the Armenian Church Council addressed all Armenian citizens who had kept photos, objects, or documents related to the tragic events, encouraging them to donate their material to the museum and thus contribute to the preservation of the memory of the Genocide (personal interview with Rupen Chavushyan, November 2010). The exhibition displays numerous artifacts and relics from the former Armenian territories. These include personal items, books, photographs, numerous table and pectoral crosses, reliquaries, chalices, handwritten Bibles, crucifixes, and much more that people were able to take with them as they fled the Ottoman Empire. Today, some of these priceless objects live a second life and are arranged in the museum exhibition in the crypt of the church.

As a consequence, this memorial space became an important place where the inner and outer spaces of memory intermingle. One cannot help but notice the strength of a cultural tradition that has been physically preserved through the survival of its strongest symbols: manuscripts, books, crosses, paintings, and religious objects. These are tangible remnants of a culture wiped out from its territories by genocide one cannot help but feel empathy for. They are not inanimate objects (Badei 2009) but on the contrary, full of life and hope, and have become talismans and metaphors for the survival of the Armenian people; significantly, most of these items are precisely written, inscribed, engraved, and printed. This small space, representing a culture that has survived tragic historical blows, takes on extraordinary value by demonstrating what writing can mean to people's memories across time and space. These objects are also very often connected to the religious sphere, as the Armenian alphabet has always been associated with the Armenian Church: the letters of the alphabet decorate the artifacts and make them even more distinctive of the culture of this people.

The Armenian community thus once again proves being constructed as an ethnolinguistic and ethno-religious community. The latter was perhaps the most influential and intense way of self-definition in the past, and in it the community of supposed common antiquity corresponds to the community of believers, as some pre-modern examples confirm (Smith 2007: 327).

This site also conveys the fact that what survived the Genocide are written words that recall the millenary history of the Armenian people which cannot be silenced; furthermore, they seem to be "a testimony to an omnipresent desire for writing that searches everywhere for legible signs and everywhere traces them" (Cardona 1986: 76, my translation). Indeed, as Cardona writes, "[w]herever it was offered a surface, writing covered a wide variety of materials. The variety of materials is often worth the variety of objects; writing can cover not only the surfaces specifically intended for it, but also any commodity, and this often shows us that writing serves other purposes besides its immediate one" (Cardona 1986: 76, my translation).

The rubber stamp with the Armenian alphabet which is on display in this collection is perhaps not the typical object one would expect to see in an exhibition of mainly sacred objects, but its importance in a space of remembrance of the Armenian community becomes clear when considering a symbolic level of meaning. With it, the Armenian word was stamped on papers and documents of an Armenian dimension that existed for centuries in the Ottoman Empire, which people had to abandon. However, someone, against all odds, managed to bring this object to safety, which today, more than a century later, still conveys its "historical truth" that stands in sharp contrast with the ongoing Turkish neglect of Armenian historical cultural heritage.

The small museum is a place of strategic importance for the symbolic organization of space and the practices of self-representation of the community. Since the meaning and values of Armenian identity are inevitably linked to its alphabetic system, the place of memory seems to coincide with the place of the written word. The latter derives its unquestionable authority from the fact that it comes directly from God. In order to speak, memory needs certain points of reference that must be visible to the addressees of the message. These points of reference are, first and foremost, places and objects (Nora 1984) that, thanks to memory and as a function of it, make it possible to establish not only the abstract imaginary of belonging but also the "perceptual pillars" of collective identity—in this case, being Armenians. The same sense of reverence for this script is passed on in modernized forms, conveying an unchanging message that seems to tell us the following: "I love everything written in my alphabet."

The museum presents itself as a place where Armenian identity stands out through its tragic story of survival. This proves once again how much the existence of Armenians in the Diaspora is linked to symbols, which are implemented through images with emotional content: they also express a longing for a distant, mythicized past that has become a world lost forever, but to which constant reference is made.

What is certain is that in analyzing the written evidence of a given society and inferring its weight, social distribution, and functions, one cannot attempt to understand the attitudes of its "recipients" without considering the emotional aspect of their relationship with them. But this does not concern only the Armenian audience. I think everyone can be touched by it when admiring in this small museum the objects of Armenian-Plovdivian memory, inscribed with such unique alphabetic signs.

7.5. Linguistic and Monumental Practices at the Armenian Graveyard

When we consider the presence of writing in the context of the cemetery, it is important to remember that this place is both public and private; in a sense, it stands at the intersection of the two. For this reason, it is an extremely interesting site to examine the practices of writing and self-representation that are placed within the broader context of the positive ideology of literacy and Genocide commemoration promoted by educated elites. Since the cemetery is a place where the public and the private meet, it is possible to obtain information on the extent to which the ideals and messages disseminated regarding Armenian identity are put into practice in written and public form.

In an interview in the fall of 2010, the then head of the AGBU, Mr. Rupen Chavushyan, emphasized the importance of public places such as the cemetery for the study of the visual aspect of the Armenian language. Indeed, graves are important not only for writing but especially for reading (and thus presuppose an audience) in the place where they are located:

> Everything there is written in Armenian language, as you can see... It is important because people write down the language and thus train their skills in the written form of the language to be able to read the names. It is the most

beautiful cemetery in Plovdiv. And here is the grave of our Tutunjyans who built our school. (...) The fact that the Armenian language is so visually present in our cemetery is important because you can find so many inscriptions and everyone can read them. (Personal interview with Rupen Chavushyan, November 2010)

The Plovdiv Cemetery is thus an appropriate place to reflect on the memory of the Genocide, on the individual and collective practices of identity formation, and their relation to public writing. The graves represent a history that cannot be forgotten, for most of those buried there were Genocide survivors or descendants of those who had to leave their homeland forever. These personal histories of forced displacement indeed consecrate

Figure 7.3. Mother Armenia Monument to the Victims of the Genocide in the Armenian Cemetery, Built in 1965 [Credits: G.S.].

the cemetery, and the memories of everyone contribute to the solemnity of this site.

The Armenian cemetery is separated from the general cemetery and forms an exclusively Armenian section, the only one of its kind in Bulgaria. There is also a small church here, built in 1924 in memory of the Tomasyan family with the help of donors. A plaque in front of the building where a ritual hall is located reminds that this place was built 80 years after the 1915 tragedy to honor the victims of the Armenian Genocide. Inside the cemetery, in addition to the graves, there is an element that is extremely important for our discourse on collective memory, namely a monument to the victims of the Genocide, which was erected in 1965, the year of the 50th anniversary of the beginning of the collective tragedy. At that time, the worldwide diaspora began to commemorate this event more explicitly: in Plovdiv, on the initiative of the Armenian Church Council, with the support of local Armenians and with the help of the leaders of the Erevan Organization, this memorial work by the sculptor Hazaros Bedrosyan was erected.

There are four plaques in Armenian on the monument, including a poem by Silva Kaputikyan, a famous Armenian poetess. Another plaque bears the names of the cities in Anatolia where thousands of Armenians were annihilated, such as Urfa and Muş. On the fourth side of the pedestal, a plaque in Bulgarian reads: "In memory of the one and a half million innocent Armenians from Western Armenia and Turkey who died on the way to forced exile due to the barbaric persecutions of 1915-1918." On the eastern side of the pedestal is a sculptural group with a mother embracing a child, the embodiment of the Mother of Armenia who cared for her orphaned children. At the top of the monument there is a globe with a dove.

When members of the community visit this graveyard, personal emotions for deceased relatives combine with the collective suffering materialized in the Genocide memorial, where everyone recognizes a part of themselves, and everyone feels Armenian.

Figure 7.4. Entrance to the Armenian Graveyard [Credits: G.S.].

Upon reading the inscriptions on the tombstones, something very inter-esting becomes clear: a lot of information can be gained, not only about the names of the people buried there but also about the ideological and his-torical impact on the way their names are written. There are some graves that look very old and make a strong impression on the viewer; they are esthetically very pleasing to the eye, and the oldest date back to the 1880s when the cemetery was opened (Giligyan 2001). All the tombstones from this early period have writings in Armenian script.[53]

From the inscriptions on the later tombs, it appears that there are some significant errors in the spelling of the Armenian characters. For example, on a bilingual Armenian-Bulgarian inscription, the surname "Arsenian" is found in Bulgarian, but it does not match the Armenian version, which turns out to be "Arsents'an." The only possible explanation for this inconsistent transliteration, and a consequential one, is the following: the person who executed the inscription in Armenian must not have known Armenian alphabet very well, because it seems obvious that he or she confused the Armenian character "Ց" (the aspirated /tsʰ/) with the character Ց /j/, since these two characters resemble each other in their form in capital letters.[54]

In another tomb, the spelling of a surname in 1962 (written as "Sop'taian") and in 1980 (as "Soft'aian," the correct version of the surname, derived from the Ottoman title "softa"), do not coincide: on the first inscription, the letter "Φ" was used instead of the letter "Ֆ." This can be explained not only by the vague similarity of the letters in their capitalization in Armenian but also and especially by the fact that this Armenian letter, pronounced as /pʰ/ coincides in its graphic form with the Bulgarian letter which is read as /f/! It is the same character, that is "Φ" in the capital form, a letter that comes from the Greek alphabet. This probably led to confusion in the first person responsible for the engraving of this surname. Moreover, in the second spelling of 1980, when the Soviet Eastern Armenian orthography had already been introduced, the letter "Դ" (pronounced as /t/ in Western Armenian) is replaced by the aspirated /tʰ/ "Թ" (in both Western and Eastern Armenian), although the reasons for this are unclear. If the intention in 1980 was to be consistent with the rules of Soviet-Armenian orthography, then "Դ" should have been replaced by the letter "Տ," which is read in Eastern Armenian as a non-aspirated /t/.

---

53 I have read that there were epitaphs written in Turkish with Armenian characters in Bulgaria, but unfortunately I have not managed to find or identify them in this graveyard, which is a pity as I think they are very significant. For more on this see: Miceva 2001: 154.

54 From the Ottoman title "Softa" (Sukhta), an undergraduate in a madrasa.

In another case, the same character "Ց," previously mistaken for "Ց" in capital letters, is rendered in its lowercase form "յ" but in capital letters as "J," thus a letter that is not present in the Armenian alphabet, and in a wrong context, since the rest of the word is in capital letters. The person who made the engraving, again, most likely did not know the correct form of the letter. This was also the case with the stonemasons of classical antiquity, who were craftsmen and not philologists and therefore made mistakes, even if only in copying templates. In any case, this seems to confirm once again that knowledge of the alphabet is usually very imperfect but nevertheless does not hinder its practical and symbolic use.

All these examples suggest that the communicative function in such a context may not be the primary purpose of writing in this alphabet. As with another alphabet system such as Gothic, where a tendency to "explicitness" of the visual and detachment from the other senses has been noted, the difficulty of the script in some cases makes it seem that "it is as if the written page was to be looked at, and not read" (Mc Luhan 1962: 127).

To some extent, we could argue that the inscriptions on these tombs prove that such writing practices help to express a kind of ideographic aspect of the language that transcribes the thought (ideas) rather than the phonological content. In many cases, the presence of Armenian characters, rather than a correspondence with the sounds of the Armenian language, reveals precise ideas about a traditional Armenian identity to be preserved and thus serves as its visible symbol.[55]

A dense graphic history can emerge from a single marble testimony as technology, ideology, and practice coexist at all levels; each influences the other. Thus, it is possible to find three different spellings of the typical ending of the Armenian surname "-ian" on the same tombstone: once it is written with the letter "յ" (+ "an") (again incorrectly with a lowercase letter), another time correctly with the letter "Ց" (+ "an") in capital letters according to the Soviet orthography, and finally another time with the letter "ե" (+ "an") according to the current (post-socialist) orthography of Western Armenian. Another remarkable fact is that on a gravestone,

---

55 See: Selvelli 2021 182, 271 for a similar consideration in relation to the use of the Glagolitic alphabet by Croats in contemporary times.

Figure 7.5. Bilingual Plaque under an Image Depicting the Holy See of Ejmiatsin. [Credits: G.S.]

between the Armenian letters, I found a non-existent sign, probably invented by an engraver who was not too familiar with this writing system.

Also interesting is the case of the graves on which a red star appears, which use exclusively the Bulgarian Cyrillic alphabet. Such a choice of script can be contextualized in the years of Bulgarian communism, which were the most critical in terms of oppression of minorities (and their languages): perhaps the owners of this tombstone wanted to show their willingness to write in Bulgarian and to use the red star as a strong political symbol.

It is appropriate to view writing practices in a given alphabet as the result of the interaction between writing technologies and ideologies of literacy, which are themselves part of a larger ideological system that reflects political, economic, and cultural systems of thought. Certain ideological foundations may determine the particular technical and linguistic principles: in this case, the Armenian alphabet system or the Bulgarian Cyrillic system.

Thus, certain changes in literacy and identity practices can be inferred from the analysis of the writing on the graves of the cemetery. Writing was also invented to communicate with people who are not present and is defined by its complicity with absence (Todorov 1977: 66). In the case of the Armenian diaspora, this also concerns about the absence of the lost territories in Western Armenia (now in Turkey), and in the cemetery, of course, it is about the people who are no longer there. The inscriptions we can read allow us to transcend the boundaries of the present Armenian diaspora, helping us to experience not only "another time" but also "another space," in terms of multiple factors (Bulgarian Communism, the Soviet Union, the cities in today's Turkey, etc.) influencing the writing practices in this public and private context. In this sense, writing has the necessary function of connecting, of creating passages between worlds, between spaces and times that can thus better communicate a history of Armenian identity in all its multi-layered complexity.

8. Conclusions: Multiple Belongings and New Diaspora Dynamics

Abstract: This final chapter problematizes the issues of diaspora belongings by examining the memory and mobility practices with the "lost" homeland in the former Ottoman Empire (now Turkey) and the relationship with the Republic of Armenia. It also summarizes the main findings of this research in relation to the processes of symbolic cultivation in the diaspora, with attention to the "native" Armenian alphabet.

Keywords: Armenianness, lost homeland, Republic of Armenia, active integration

8.1. The Role of the Lost Homeland and of the Republic of Armenia

For many years, the discourse on the Armenian diaspora has focused on the notion of "impermanence": from this perspective, life in a foreign land was a temporary and transitory phase before the longed-for return to the motherland (Tölölyan 2002: 49). While waiting, Armenians committed themselves to supporting their community's identity and survival in various ways. This imperative emerged after the Genocide and has been reflected in the discourses and ideologies of some political parties in the host countries of the world diaspora (Aghanian 2007: 118). For example, writer Suren Vetsigian did not let go of the dream of returning to the old homeland for a long time, as we read in an excerpt from his diary from 1932:

> Armenia now belongs to Turkey, with all the Armenians dead or scattered abroad. But God will do us justice. No nation will enjoy the spoils got in unjust way. [...] I hope, before I die, to see the day when the boundaries that divide the nations have disappeared, as it happened in Soviet Russia. That in the near future Armenians will be able to go back to their fatherland, I have no doubt about it. (Vetsigian 2014: 102)

In a sense, the myth of the return (Safran 1991) provided the diaspora with a source of hope and a sense of destiny, as well as an ideological justification for its institutional structures. Of course, myths are not the same as "fictional stories" but rather images, words, and narratives that can evoke more than mere facts. They have a symbolic power and create a magnified imaginary of the past. The bitter story of the lost lands of the ancestors became a myth for Armenians that was "remembered, narrated, and used, that is, woven into the fabric of the present" (Assman 1997: 9–10). Therefore, in the collective memory of the Armenian people, these narratives acquired a value that went beyond mere historiography.

Nevertheless, despite the collapse of the Soviet Union and the establishment of an independent Armenian state, very few Armenians of the diaspora came from around the world to settle in the new country (Panossian 1998: 169, Kasbarian 2015). On the contrary, many left the newly independent Armenia to live elsewhere. Some of them came to Bulgaria, in a process that has not stopped until today.

When Armenians in the diaspora refer to the desire of returning to their homeland, they are engaged in a process of "double imagination" (Panossian 1998: 163, Aghanian 2007: 166). The majority of them, indeed, have their genetic roots in the Western Armenian towns and cities, as well as other parts of the former Ottoman Empire, where their ancestors lived until the Genocide of 1915–1918. Consequently, their "true homeland" is in present-day Turkey: in Anatolia, Thrace, and Istanbul, to which they would find it very difficult to return.

Instead, some diaspora Armenians, descendants of people who escaped the Genocide, decide to travel to the Republic of Armenia. They perceive this trip as a kind of pilgrimage, a symbolic approach to a part of their "imaginary homeland," but this does not change the fact that the territory of today's Republic of Armenia is only a small percentage of the land where Armenians used to live in the past. The independent Republic of Armenia is the first state for Armenians in many centuries. It maintains special relations with the Armenian diaspora throughout the world, including through the figure of the High Commissioner for Diaspora Affairs (formerly Ministry of the Diaspora, see Vardanyan 2021: 91), and has officially defined the Armenian nation as encompassing the diaspora of the world, a policy that resonates with the sentiments of many Armenians (Tölölyan & Papazian 2014).

Defining the contemporary Armenian diaspora is particularly challenging, since this constitutes a "diaspora of diasporas" (Brubaker 2005) that is geographically dispersed and spans several generations. However, if we had to find a common feature to define the experience of being part of this community, it would be the special sense of the past. This feeds on a "myth of return" (Safran 1991) that in some ways characterizes the experience of diaspora communities through nostalgic feelings (Vardanyan 2021: 44). The institutions of the "old world" are idealized and the geography of the motherland is sentimentalized (Aghanian 2007: 33). For this reason, too, one sometimes has the impression that, although the Republic of Armenia appears to have evolved and gone forward, the diaspora communities continue to cling strongly to pre-diasporic customs and structures, seeing themselves as custodians of the national heritage.

To some extent, as one informant confirmed to me, this is also a reason why the "newcomers" from the Republic of Armenia often do not manage to integrate well with the "oldcomers" in Plovdiv. As mentioned before, there are indeed several cultural discrepancies between the two groups, as well as language differences. "They live in a kind of stuck past, a timeless dimension where they repeat the same things and are almost afraid of change, moreover, they tend to marry only among themselves, while in Armenia there are many more mixed marriages!" an informant told me.

The Armenians of the "old diaspora" feed on memories that are handed down and re-signified from time to time, and most of them have never experienced Armenia other than as the "Armenia of the mind." In their imagination, we find the irretrievably lost places in today's Turkey rather than the perspective of the vibrant and dynamic Yerevan (see also Kasbarian 2015). As remarked by Robin Cohen (1997: 4), diasporas are forced in a discourse on themselves which provides "an opportunity to construct and define their own historical experience, to invent their tradition."

Although I do not believe that tradition is actually "invented" (Hobsbawm & Ranger 1983) by the Armenians, since it was already present in certain elements that remained essentially unchanged (Vardanyan 2021: 44), it is nevertheless true that historical cultural elements of a nation are elaborated and re-actualized by the educational elites according to the contingencies of the moment. This symbolic capital is useful to express certain values and identity policies considered crucial. Cultural identity is not fixed and homogeneous; there are several creative processes within a given social group, although the same Armenians often tend to think of themselves in "essentialist" terms (Tchilingirian 2018) as a distinct cultural group with fixed origins and distinct cultural characteristics. In addition, cultural identity is not something given once and for all and does not consist of an unchanged origin to which one can return absolutely and definitively. "Of course, it is not a mere phantasm either. It is something—not a mere trick of the imagination. It has its histories—and histories have their real, material and symbolic effects. The past (...) is always constructed through memory, fantasy, narrative and myth" (Hall 1990: 226).

Similar to Stuart Hall's definition of Africa, the old Armenian homeland belongs to an imaginary geography and history in the minds of diaspora Armenians. However, the territories in present-day Turkey inhabited by the ancestors before the Genocide have more than imaginary or figurative value, as they have tangible effects for members of the diaspora and generate real actions.[56] Some of these effects are also important elements in the practice of transmitting cultural memory and elaborating the postmemory of the Genocide. Examples of this in the Armenian community of Plovdiv are the trips organized by the associations connected with the Armenian Church to Edirne, the first Turkish city after the border with Bulgaria. Edirne and other towns in Turkish Thrace (such as Rodosto, Malgara, Çorlu) hosted large Armenian communities before the Genocide, and many survivors passed from here on their way to Bulgaria.[57] In particular, Rodosto (Tekirdağ) is a name that recurs very often in the narratives and personal stories of the descendants of the survivors (see Kevorkyan 2019). An active group of pensioners shows enthusiasm for such trips and travels to Edirne quite frequently, despite the unpleasant travel conditions, especially the strict and lengthy customs controls at the busy Bulgarian/Turkish border of Kapıkule. It is interesting to note that some of these elderly descendants of Genocide survivors participating in the journey are trilingual; they are among the few remaining Armenians who speak Turkish in addition to Armenian and Bulgarian. They, indeed,

---

56 On the practice of "diaspora tourism" see, for example, Turan & Bakalian 2015.
57 See: the trilogy by the Bulgarian-Armenian writer Sevda Sevan, partly set here: *Rodosto, Rodosto, Njakăde na Balkanite, Der Zor: Roman-trilogija*.

heard this language spoken at home from their parents or grandparents who came from different parts of the Ottoman Empire and sometimes spoke Turkish to them. In other cases, they used it as a "secret language" so as not to be understood by their children or grandchildren, but this did not prevent them from learning it (interview with Lusona Cherchiayan in August 2021). Even today, the Turkish language is in some ways taboo, but these women over 70 are still very aware of the Ottoman heritage of such linguistic competences and, of course, don't want to associate them with Turkey itself, but rather with a common multiethnic world of the past. In many cases, though, they actively use Turkish when they travel to this country.

The AGBU branch in Plovdiv frequently publishes articles about the trips of Plovdiv Armenians to the historical areas of Western Armenia in Eastern Turkey. For example, in 2015, a column entitled "A Journey Through Our Ancient Land" appeared in several issues of the AGBU newspaper on the occasion of the first centenary of the Genocide and has continued over the years in the time of the year around April 24 (e.g., also in numbers 222–223, 2019). In this series of articles, the journalists and members of the Armenian community of Plovdiv describe the Armenian cultural heritage of cities such as Kars, Diyarbakır, and Van. They point out the poverty in the region and the conversion of historic Armenian sites into Muslim sites, as well as the lack of recognition of the Armenian component of cultural heritage, as the ethnonym "Armenian" is completely absent from the signs describing the sites. An example of this is the cultural heritage in the city of Van, the first historical Armenian capital: "Everywhere it is mentioned that the architecture of Van is Urartian, and nowhere does it say that it is of Armenian origin" (number 223, page 7). However, this also occurs in the city of Ani and in the Church of Surp Arak'elots (Holy Apostoles Church) in Kars, which now serves as a mosque, both located in Northeastern Turkey. Other historical sites described in the travelogues published in the AGBU Bulletin include the Armenian village of Vakıflı (the only remaining Armenian village in Turkey with a population of about 135 near the mountain of Musa Dag, (Musa Ler in Armenian), the cities of Kayseri, Iskenderun, Antakya, Adana, and Tarsus, all of which were visited to commemorate the 104th anniversary of the beginning of the Armenian Genocide (number 230, page 2). The trips to the cities in today's Turkey made by Plovdiv Armenians can be interpreted not only as a response to the history of physical extermination and forcible expulsion of their ancestors from the ancient lands but also as a response to the country's continued denial of the rights of the survivors and their descendants to return to their ancient homeland or to have confiscated property returned to them. Living so close to the Turkish border (2 hours away) gives the Plovdiv diaspora a "privileged" position. They are close enough to the successor state of the Ottoman Empire to visit it, but at the same time, they are more exposed to a painful confrontation with the past and the relentless denial of the Genocide by many different Turkish actors.

8.2. Challenges and Resources of the Diasporic Life

The survival of the complex memory of the past in diaspora communities depends to a great extent on the active role of specialists and others in maintaining a sense of collective distinction and mission. In the Armenian case, this is realized by nurturing the myths of origin and the distinctive symbols that are seen as helping to define the special character of the nation. This representative elite is the one that engages in the social sphere to perpetuate traditional ideals and values through various initiatives, whether in the form of articles in the periodical press, lectures by teachers, or, as we have just seen, by organizing excursions to significant historical sites. The reason for using symbolic resources, in fact, is to motivate ideologies and collective actions (Smith 2009: 16). The initiatives of the defenders of a specific Armenian identity in the diaspora are based on the acceptance of a specific symbolic framework that is activated at certain moments of interaction between members of the community. Elements such as the Armenian Genocide, the Armenian martyr, the lost homeland, the language and its unique alphabet, or the Armenian Apostolic Church gain strength through their representation as symbols and, at the same time, through the fact that they are partially subjective and thus become ideal means through which people can communicate on a common basis. Individuality and sociality are reconciled in this way: symbols are visible to all and clear in their meaning and are then also experienced in a personal way.

Because of its crucial role in strengthening internal cohesion and promoting a unified collective memory, symbolism serves to unite different social classes and level the collective consciousness through the use of ancestral discourses and objects related to primary knowledge, and to arouse immediate emotions. Memory, indeed, "is one of the sites of ideology and, through the representation of the past that it provides, helps to justify the present and shape the future from a social perspective" (Petrucci 2007: 116, my translation).

From the distance of their diaspora dimension, Armenians generally feel a strong sense of belonging to their ethnic culture, are proud of their historical heritage, and, above all, exhibit strong "cultural longevity." This indicates that special forces are at work to preserve the basic characteristics that constitute being Armenian across time and space. Nevertheless, younger generations of Armenians experience their relationship to Armenian heritage in ways that do not always conform to the essentialist and ascriptive expectations on the collective identity of older generations. Their lives are characterized by higher levels of cultural hybridity, new terms of comparison in the European context and beyond, and forms of personal reappropriation of Armenian elements that nurture subjective and dynamic visions of Armenianness (Tchilingirian 2018).

The concept of the Armenian diaspora forces us to reject a discourse still based on the dichotomy of national and non-national and emphasizes the ability to combine resources and networks from multiple (transnational) locations to maximize the freedom and independence from the boundaries of each nation-state (Aghanian 2007: VI).

Conceptualizing the Armenian diaspora experience in terms of transnationalism, multiple identities, and "in-betweenness" thus, challenges the widely held notion that certain groups and their cultures somehow belong to one territory and opens the door to a broader and more complex conception of identity. The specificity of the diaspora condition provides Armenians with the opportunity to feel part of a larger communicative system and to be connected with many contexts: the host country, the Republic of Armenia, the lost homeland in present-day Turkey, and other Armenian communities around the world.

In the multiethnic context of Plovdiv, Armenians and Bulgarians prove to be, in a sense, allies in dealing with the Islamic heritage in the country, in a logic of identification based on a history characterized by common elements of subordination to the Muslim *millet* during the long period of the Ottoman Empire. As mentioned, the attitude of Armenians toward Turks is sometimes characterized by elements of mistrust, due to the persistent denial of the Armenian Genocide by their representatives, although contradictory attitudes are triggered by the fact that knowledge of the Turkish language and its culture still exists in the older generations. The latter proves to be very similar to Armenian in some respects (food, music, etc.). For example, one fact that really struck me was that all the retired ladies, when they met at the clubhouse on Tuesdays, were systematically captured by a Turkish soap opera and constantly praised its virtues. I had the impression that they felt very familiar with the Turkish context of the series because they recognized (or idealized) in it the elements of a common world of the past, that is, similar sociocultural characteristics dating back to the Ottoman heritage. Politically, the issue of the unfavorable relations with Turkey plays an important role in the discussions of Armenian intellectuals in Plovdiv and, above all, in the local newspapers, especially in the weekly *Vahan*, which promotes the circulation of articles dealing with the struggle for the recognition of the Armenian Genocide by the Turkish government and other states of the world. This newspaper's articles very often deal with the Nagorno-Karabakh (Artsakh in Armenian) war, in which Armenia clashed with Azerbaijan in the late 1980s, an issue that has tragically resurfaced in 2020 (Vardanyan 2021: 22), and had further tragic developments in September 2023, with the forced departure of over 100,000 Armenians from this region. This conflict represents a kind of reactualization of the problem of the territorial claims Armenia makes against the "Turkic" world, and thus, its narrative in the Plovdiv context draws on many symbolic resources set in a complicated war setting that has become a new backdrop for the projection of old myths and expectations.

In the daily life of Armenians in Plovdiv, however, the greatest "threat" comes not from Turkey or Azerbaijan but from the danger of linguistic assimilation. The fears of the defenders of the Armenian language are based on the assessment of the impact of the globalization processes, which significantly affect the preservation of diasporic identity, language, and culture. The undeniable problem is that the Western branch of the Armenian language is losing speakers in the diaspora at a high rate, and the challenge is to ensure an appropriate institutional role for this language in the long term. More than 1600 years after the creation of the Armenian alphabet by Mesrop Mashtots, the alarming danger of assimilation seems to be more topical than ever, since the national language and alphabet have little practical use in this Balkan country. Indeed, in the daily life of this community, this "mother tongue", together with the old customs and traditions, is relegated to limited and internal spaces, mainly to family relations, Armenian cultural and recreational clubs, and religious institutions. Thus, speaking and reading the Armenian language, participating in Armenian cultural or social events, and being involved in the spiritual life of the community are viewed by the local Armenian intelligentsia as a goal to be achieved, a duty to be fulfilled, and an ethical imperative to "stay Armenian" (Manoukian 1986: 80). The cultivation of a sense of "distinctiveness" is a fundamental aspect of the life of diaspora communities, without which they risk being completely assimilated by the host context (Manoukian 1986: 80). This explains the attention paid by the local media to issues related to the language and the alphabet, interpreting their value in light of the challenges of contemporary diaspora society. Here is a particularly explicit contribution to the discourse on the survival of Armenian identity, published in the *Parekordzagani Tzain*, whose title is "Speak Armenian."

> Many world historians and scholars have tried to explain the enigma: How could a small nation, which had no great military force, withstand so many vicissitudes without disappearing from the face of the earth, but rather be reborn? One explanation for this mystery is probably rooted in a characteristic feature of the Armenian people—their devotion to their mother tongue, literature and spiritual culture. Where the people cannot win with the sword, writing continues to win from generation to generation, building up its weapons, hopes and faith. (Parekordzagani Tzain 2006: 4)

Armenians perceive their culture and history as strongly shaped by the power of the written word, their culture being one that particularly favors the written form of the language. For this reason, the educated elites of the diaspora emphasize the value of Armenian writing, affirming that it has been, and can continue to be, a powerful weapon in the hands of the people in their struggle for a glorious future. At the end of the same article in the *Parekordzagan Tzain*, we then read:

> So that we do not forget who we are, in what language our grandparents spoke and what wisdom they left us, let us speak Armenian, let us write Armenian, let us

think Armenian, let us live the Armenian way! This is our goal. (Parekordzagani Tzain 2006: 4)

The active maintenance of this tradition in the present becomes a question of crucial ethical importance for being Armenian: the situation in the past, when various foreign nations threatened the existence of this people, is seen as comparable to the present condition of the diaspora, in which Armenians are scattered to all corners of the world and are exposed to a variety of potentially assimilating influences.

8.3. Cybernetic Considerations

A society can (...) be considered as a cybernetic (macro) model, with its own self-regulatory mechanisms and internal levels of structuring (or micromodels). (...) The maintenance of social order (...) presupposes that society is preserved among its members, that there is a continuous production of ideological forms and that these circulate (...) and reinforce or modify what society considers positive values at that moment. (Cardona 2009: 64, my translation)

Cybernetic theory helps us to visualize society as an organism: a complex living system based on dynamic balances. For this reason, its behavior can be described as characterized by aspects of closure and openness, which allow it to survive and evolve. The former, the aspects of closure, aim at keeping the internal organization strictly intact, viewed as a set of relationships between the components that form a composite unit (Maturana & Varela 1984: 17). The latter, on the other hand, the aspects of openness, are to be understood in terms of necessary exchanges with the environment aimed at supplying itself with energy, a set of relations through which the organization of the system in a given environment manifests itself as a particular space-time entity.

In what sense can we speak of the aspects of openness and closure in relation to the life of the Armenian community in Plovdiv? I believe that the preservation of the internal organization, the hard and unchanging core of the ethnic identity, is possible precisely through a continuous dissemination of the "ethnogenic" discourse, which consists of symbolic elements connected with the sphere of myth, imagination, and emotions—in short, to a certain extent of irrationality, metaphor, and, thus, transcontextuality (Bateson 1972: 272).

On the other hand, as far as openness is concerned, I believe that the appropriation and application of patterns and elements related to the Bulgarian context, for example, in the choice of language in which books or newspapers are written, prove to be a necessary measure to avoid forms of self-ghettoization or isolation and thus the risk of a slow suffocation of energies which are essential for survival. If we consider the conservative aspects of the Armenian community's actions, we find that the space of writing offers itself as a privileged symbolic place. Those who actively use it, such as journalists, writers, poets, and teachers, play a fundamental role in familiarizing community members with the discourse of identity since the alphabet is one of its most important symbols. As we have seen, this writing system is used both in the practical dimension as a means of writing and on the "mythopoetic" level as the subject of a narrative about chosenness and distinctiveness. In connection with the dimension of the national, the element of writing thus acquires a strategic importance both for the common imaginary and for communicative functionality.

The Armenian alphabet is much more than just a system of signs: behind and within it is a history of vital importance to the Armenian people. This is linked to the history of a long dispersion to the most diverse places in the world, during which Armenians carried their symbols and myths with them and kept their identity alive, never giving in to the dynamics of assimilation or isolation (Payaslian 2010) but creating a positive example of "active integration" (Zekiyan 2000: 165), which has been called "the Armenian paradigm of survival" (ib.).

In Plovdiv, Armenians represent a small community (around 2,000 people out of about 340,000 total inhabitants), but as is typical of most Armenians in the diaspora, despite their long residence in the host country and their successful integration, they refuse to identify only with the country in which they live. Rather, they express patterns of multiple belonging, they harbor a "longing" for their lost homeland, and they are in contact with other Armenian communities around the world through supranational organizations of various kinds. They thus experience a "multilocal" condition, which has also shaped its past in terms of polycentrism (Tölölyan, 1996, Zekiyan 1997a). I have defined this tool as a kind of dual, binocular vision of "non-exclusive belonging" (Selvelli 2017: 69) that requires knowing how to be able to enter and exit different contexts (Bateson 1972: 79–81).

> As far as relations and interaction between cultures are concerned, in the sense of the desired ethnocultural pluralism, Armenians, in our opinion, have a message of their own to convey, a model to propose by virtue of their historical vocation as a frontier people, a bridge, a catalyst or, perhaps with a happier expression, an elixir of life that flows everywhere and in the most diverse latitudes, creating circulation of energies, contacts, exchanges and mutual enrichment between peoples and cultures. This is certainly one of the most fascinating aspects of the historical vocation and destiny of the Armenian people. (Zekiyan 2000: 141, my translation)

Armenian communities around the world distinguish themselves by being well integrated into the host country: they are usually very well educated, included in the workforce, and proficient in the national language as well as foreign languages. Such was the precondition for the creation of a multifaceted and polycentric identity pattern, corresponding to the concept defined by Zekiyan (1997b and 2000: 141) of identité polyvalent ("versatile identity"). The gradual integration of Armenians into the daily life of the host countries is accompanied by a parallel movement of ideal and symbolic reunification with tradition and the community of origin (Payaslian 2010): this process allows communities to recognize themselves in a national destiny and belonging even after decades. It is possible to observe that the discourse of belonging to the dimension of Armenian identity is forged through the interchange between the initiatives of the elites and the responses of the public, which can accept, reject, or reform such identity projects. In this respect, "symbolic" (see Bakalian 1993: 6–7) Armenianness is the specific choice that is made, in terms of cultivating a personal, non-ascriptive feeling of belonging.

As we have seen, the validity of the alphabet symbol as a form of knowledge about Armenian identity does not depend on the extent to which individuals understand it in its technical function (through reading and writing competences): the symbolism is transparent in its entirety, but members of society are content to participate in it to some extent, each to varying degrees and in their own way. This writing system often exerts an influence on the reader or viewer through its esthetic value: the image of the alphabet can act as a symbol affecting both the individual and collective consciousness and elevating it to a higher level of abstraction (Arnheim 1969: 166).

Those who have come into contact with Armenian culture know how much emotional value lies behind each of those characters, which embody the story of the emergence of a people that has allowed it to live on in different and unpredictable ways.

It is presented as the form of a cherished and revered collectivity, as an element of memory that helps to ensure a sense of continuity with past generations. Memory itself is equated with the medium of writing through the image of imprinting, of writing something down in memory. "For just as what is written is fixed in the form of letters on wax, so what is entrusted to memory is imprinted in places as on a wax tablet or on the page; and the memory of things is preserved through images as if they were letters" (Martianus Capella[58] cited in Cardona 2009: 109, my translation). The metaphor proves perfect for this diasporic context, and so the memory of being Armenian is also fixed through images that use the letters of the Armenian alphabet and weave a story that has so much more to tell, beyond the one I have written here.

It all started just like that for me, with an image of Armenian characters that aroused my curiosity and prompted me to test their power over me: because of this impression, which was undoubtedly very irrational, I wanted to follow them and see where they wanted to lead me. I have not regretted it.

> How dear is your ominous tongue,/ Your coffins are rough and young,/ Where the letters are blacksmith's tongs,/ And each word is a cramp... (Osip Mandel'štam, Journey to Armenia).

---

58 Late-Antiquity Latin prose writer.

Bibliography

Adalian, R.P. (2013). "The Armenian Genocide". In S. Totten & W.S. Parsons (eds.), *Centuries of Genocide. Essays and Eyewitness Accounts.* New York-London: Routledge, 117–156.

Adjemian, B. & Nichanian, M. (2018). "Repenser les 'massacres hamidiens': la question du precedent". In *Études arméniennes contemporaines* 10, 7–18.

AGBU. (2015). "The Armenian language as an endangered language in Europe. A contribution to the European Roadmap for Linguistic Diversity". *AGBU Europe.* Available at: https://agbueurope.org/wp-content/uploads/sites/17/2015/12/Contribution-to-the-NPLD-Roadmap-for-Language-Diversity-Armenian-AGBU-Europe-and-C.-Gulbenkian.pdf [8 March 2023].

Aghanian, D. (2007). *The Armenian Diaspora: Cohesion and Fracture.* Lanham: University Press of America.

Agukyan, S. A. (1995). *Otzvucite na Armenskija Genocid v Bălgarskija Pečat.* Sofia: Publication of the National Committee "80 Years from the Armenian Genocide".

Akçam, T. (2018). *Killing Orders.* London: Palgrave Macmillan.

Anderson, B. (1991). *Imagined Communities. Reflections on the Origin and Spread of Nationalism.* London-New York: Verso, 1991 [1986].

Arakelyan, T. (2015). "The role of language in the preservation of Armenian identity". In *Scripta Neophilologica Posnaniensia* XV, 7–12.

Arnaudov, V. (2001). "Pavlikjanstvoto – armenskata eres, i negovoto vlijanie v bălgarskite zemi". In. G. Hayrabedyan (ed.), *Bălgari i Armenci zaedno prez vekovete.* Sofia: Tangra.

Arnheim, R. (1969). *Visual Thinking.* Berkeley: University of California Press.

Artinyan, K. (2000). *Sledovnici na Amirdovlat Amasiatsi. Plovdivskite medici, stomatolozi i farmacevti armenci i potomci na armenci.* Plovdiv: Armen Tur.

Aslanian, D. (1993). *Histoire de la Bulgarie de l'antiquité à nos jours.* Versailles: Trimontium.

Aslanian, S. D. (2011). *From the Indian Ocean to the Mediterranean: The Global Trade Networks of Armenian Merchants from New Julfa.* Berkeley: University of California Press.

Assmann, J. (1997). *Moses the Egyptian: The Memory of Egypt in Western Monotheism.* Cambridge: Harvard University Press.

Assmann, J. (2008). "Communicative and cultural memory". In A. Erll & A. Nünning (eds.), *Cultural Memory Studies: An International and Interdisciplinary Handbook.* Berlin: De Gruyter, 109–118.

Badei, R. (2009). *La vita delle cose.* Roma: Laterza.

Bakalian, A. (1993). *Armenian-Americans: From Being to Feeling Armenian.* New Brunswick, NJ: Transaction Publishers.

Barby, H. (1917). *Au Pays de l'Épouvante. L'Arménie Martyre.* Paris.

Barth, F. (1998). "Introduction". In F. Barth (ed.), *Ethnic Groups and Boundaries.* Prospect Heights: Waveland Press, 9–37 [1969].

Barton, D. & Papen, U. (2010). "What is the anthropology of writing?" In: D. Barton & U. Papen (eds.), *The Anthropology of Writing. Understanding Textually Mediated Worlds.* London: Continuum, 3–26.

Bateson, G. (1972). *Steps to an Ecology of Mind.* Chicago: University of Chicago Press.

Berberyan, Y. (2019). "Vstăpitelni dumi". In: Y. Konstantinova & I. Načev (eds.), *S pogled kăm Amerika: Izsledvaneto na bălgarski armenci ot socialističeska Bălgarija.* Sofia: Fakel, 5–18.

Beroujon, A. (2010). "Lawful and unlawful writings in Lyon in the seventeenth century". In D. Barton & U. Papen (eds.), *The Anthropology of Writing. Understanding Textually Mediated Worlds.* London: Continuum, 190–213.

Bid Book. (2019). *Plovdiv Together.* Plovdiv: Foundation Zaedno.

Bjorklund, U. (2003). "Armenians of Athens and Istanbul: The Armenian diaspora and the 'transnational' nation". In *Global Networks* 3 (3), 337–354.

Bohosyan, M. (1999). *I sleze Noj ot Ararat. Armenski mitove, legendi i predanija.* Plovdiv: Armen Tur.

Bolognesi, G. (2000). "Presentazione". In B. L. Zekiyan, *L'Armenia e gli armeni.* Milano: Guerini e associati, 1–10.

Boyajian, L. & Grigorian, H. (1986). "Psychosocial Sequelae of the Armenian Genocide". In S. R. Graubard (ed.), *The Armenian Genocide in Perspective*. New York: Routledge.

Brubaker, R. (2005). The "diaspora" diaspora. In *Ethnic and Racial Studies* 28 (1), 1–19.

Cardona, G. R. (1982). "Introduzione". In *La Ricerca Folklorica* 5, 3–7.

Cardona, G. R. (1986). *Storia universale della scrittura*. Milano: Mondadori.

Cardona, G. R. (2009). *Antropologia della scrittura*. Torino: Utet [1981].

Castellan, G. (1991). *Histoire des Balkans*. Paris: Fayard.

Chahinian, T. & Bakalian, A. (2015). "Language in Armenian American communities: Western Armenian and efforts for preservation". In *International Journal of the Sociology of Language* 237 (1), 37–57.

Chai, S. K. (2005). "Predicting ethnic boundaries". In *European Sociological Review* 21 (4), 375–391.

Chavushyan, R. (2004). "Soobštenie do obštnostta". In *Parekordzagani Tzain* 1: 1–2.

Clifford, J. & Marcus, G. (1986). *Writing Culture: Poetics and Politics of Ethnography*. Berkeley CA: University of California Press.

Cohen, A. P. (1985). *Symbolic Construction of Community*. London: Tavistock.

Cohen, R. (1997). *Global Diasporas*. London: Routledge.

Dadrian, V. N. (1995). *The History of the Armenian Genocide. Ethnic Conflict from the Balkans to Anatolia to the Caucasus*. New York: Berghahn Books.

Dagher-Margosian, M. (2021). "Cooking as Resistance: Liana Aghajanian on Food & Armenian Survival". In *Asia Art Tours* (online). Available at: https://asiaarttours.com/cooking-as-resistance-liana-aghajanian-on-food-armenian-survival/ [8 March 2023].

Dashtents, K. (2003). *Zovăt na oračite*. Plovdiv: Armen Tur.

De Certeau, M. (2005). *La scrittura dell'altro*. Milano: Cortina.

Der-Garabedian, H. S. (2004). *Jail to Jail: Autobiography of a Survivor of the 1915 Armenian Genocide*. New York: iUniverse.

Dermeguerian, R. (1997). "Espaces de fonctionnement des deux branches de l'armenien litteraire moderne". In J. Dum-Tragut (ed.), *Die armenische Sprache in der Europäischen Diaspora*. Grazer Linguistische Monographien, 19–35.

De Saussure, F. (1959). *Course in General Linguistics*. New York: The Philosophical Library. [1916].

Deukmejian, G. (1992). "Introduction". In R. G. Hovannisian (ed.), *The Armenian Genocide: History, Politics, Ethics*. Basingstoke: Macmillan, 1–8.

Dink, H. (2011). *Dva blizki naroda, dva dalečni săseda Armenija – Turcija*. Plovdiv: Parekordzagan.

Donabedian-Demopoulos, A. (2018). "Middle East and beyond - Western Armenian at the crossroads: A sociolinguistic and typological sketch". In B. Christiane (ed.), *Linguistic Minorities in Turkey and Turkic-Speaking Minorities of the Periphery*. Wiesbaden: Harrassowitz Verlag, 89–148.

Drost Abgarian, A. (1997). "Perspektiven der Spracherhaltung in Deutschland". In J. Dum-Tragut (ed.), *Die armenische Sprache in der Europäischen Diaspora*. Grazer Linguistische Monographien, 165–176.

Drücker, J. (1995). *The Alphabetic Labyrinth: The Letters in History and Imagination*. New York: Thames and Hudson.

Dufoix, S. (2008). *Diaspora*. Berkeley: University of California Press.

Eriksen, T. (2001). *Small Places, Large Issues. An Introduction to Social and Cultural Anthropology*. London: Pluto Press [1995].

Erniasyan, H. (2005). "90 godini ot armenskija genocid. Hronika na otzivite ot săbitieto". In *Parekordzagani Tzain* 65, 4.

Erniasyan, H. (2010). "Praznikăt na predovača". In *Parekordzagani Tzain* 70, 2.

Erniasyan, H. (ed.) (2019). *V sveta na armenskata kuhnja*. Plovdiv: Parekordzagan.

Fabietti, U. (2004). *L'identità etnica. Storia di un concetto equivoco*. Roma: Carocci [1995].

Ferrari, A. (2003). *L'Ararat e la gru. Studi sulla storia e cultura degli armeni*. Milano: Mimesis.

Ferrari, A. (2016). "Viaggio nei luoghi della memoria armena in Turchia e Azerbaigian". In *LEA – Lingue e letterature d'Oriente e d'Occidente* 5, 179–192.

Ferrari, A. (2016b). *Armenia. Una cristianità di frontiera*. Rimini: Il Cerchio.

Ferrari, A. (2016c). "Van: il Paradiso Perduto degli Armeni". In M. Guidetti & S. Mondini (eds.), *A mari usque ad mare. Cultura visuale e materiale dall'Adriatico all'India. Scritti in memoria di Gianclaudio Macchiarella*. Venezia: Venezia University Press, 317–335.

Ferrari, A. (2019). *L'Armenia perduta. Viaggio nella memoria di un popolo*. Roma: Salerno Editrice.

Field, T. T. (2001). "Literacy and language ideologies in a European situation of language loss". In T. Ammerlaan, (ed.), *Sociolinguistic and Psycholinguistic Perspectives on Maintenance and Loss of Minority Languages*. Munster: Waxmann, 93–108.

Fishman, J. (1977). "Introduction". In J. Fishman (ed.), *Advances in the Creation and Revision of Writing Systems*. The Hague: Mouton, 11–27.

Fishman, J. A. (1991). *Reversing Language Shift*. Clevedon: Multilingual Matters.

Fırat, D. Şannan, B., Muti, Ö., Gürpınar, Ö., & Özkaya. F. (2017). "Postmemory of the Armenian Genocide: A Comparative Study of the 4th Generation in Turkey and Armenia". In *Oral History/Forum d'histoire orale* 37 (Special Issue on Generations and Memory: Continuity and Change), online version: http://www.oralhistoryforum.ca/index.php/ohf /article/view/626/70

Fraenkel, B. (2010). "Writing acts: when writing is doing". In D. Barton & U. Papen (eds.), *The Anthropology of Writing. Understanding Textually Mediated Worlds*. London: Continuum, 3–32.

Garabedyan, A. (2001). "Sătrudničestvo i sǎvmetsni dejstvija meždu armenskoto i bǎlgarskoto osvoboditelno dviženie v kraja na XIX i načaloto na XX vek". In G. Hayrabedyan (ed.), *Bǎlgari i Armenci zaedno prez vekovete*. Sofia: Tangra, 331–359.

Garabedyan, A. (2001b). "Formirane na armenskata obštnost i nejnata rolja v razvitieto na bǎlgarskata dǎržava". In G. Hayrabedyan (ed.), *Bǎlgari i Armenci zaedno prez vekovete*. Sofia: Tangra, 231–268.

Gaunt, D. (2014). "Memory is more important than death and Life': 100 Years after the Armenian Genocide". In *Baltic Worlds* 7 (2–3), 9–11.

Gavrilova, R. (1999). *Bulgarian Urban Culture in the Eighteenth and Nineteenth Centuries*. Selinsgrove: Susquehanna University Press.

Giligyan, A. (2001). "Armenski nadgrobija v Plovdiv prez XVII-XIX vek". In *Godišnik na arheologičeskija Muzej – Plovdiv* 10, 139–149.

Giligyan, A. (2002). *Stranici iz istorijata na armenskata kolonija v Plovdiv i nejnata cărkva Surp Kevork.* Plovdiv: Adg.

Grace, D. M. (2007). *Relocating Consciousness. Diasporic Writers and the Dynamics of Literary Experience.* Amsterdam-New York: Brill.

Grosby, S. (2005). *Nationalism: A Very Short Introduction.* Oxford: Oxford University Press.

Gueriguian, J. L. (1997). "Essential western Armenian semantic units: Object, methods and finality". In J. Dum-Tragut (ed.), *Die armenische Sprache in der Europäischen Diaspora.* Grazer Linguistische Monographien, 137–164.

Gulesserian, L. A. (2015). *Because If the Dead Cannot Live, Neither Do We': Postmemory and Passionate Remembering in Micheline Aharonian Marcom's Armenian Genocide Trilogy.* Ph.D. dissertation. Austin: University of Texas at Austin.

Gul, K. & Duygu. (2018). "100 Voices after 100 years: Remembering the Armenian Genocide in Diaspora". In *Popular Communication* 16 (2), 128–140.

Haigaz, A. (1935). *The Fall of the Aerie.* Boston: Ararat Publisher.

Hall, S. (1990). "Cultural identity and diaspora". In J. Rutherford (ed.), *Identity, Community, Culture, Future.* London: Lawrence & Wishart, 222–237.

Hamamdjian, V. (2004). *Vahan's Triumph: Autobiography of an Adolescent Survivor of the Armenian Genocide.* New York: iUniverse.

Hamilton, J. & Hamilton, B. (1998). *Christian Dualist Heresies in the Byzantine World, c.650-c.1450.* Manchester: Manchester University Press.

Haroutyunian, S. (2015). "Echoes of the Armenian Genocide in literature and cinema". In *Annali di Ca' Foscari. Serie Orientale* 51: 43–58.

Hassiotis, I. K. (2002). "The Armenians". In: R. Clogg (ed.), *Minorities in Greece: Aspects of a Plural Society.* London: C. Hurst & Co. Publishers, 94–111.

Hayrabedyan, G. (1994). "Armenskijat periodičen pečat v Bălgarija". In *Bălgarska Etnografija* 3–4, 100–109.

Hirsch, M. (2008). "Generation of Postmemory". In *Poetics Today* XXIX (1), 103–128.

Hobsbawm, E. & Ranger, T. (ed.) (1983). *The Invention of Tradition*. Cambridge: Cambridge University Press.

Holslag, A. (2018). *The Transgenerational Consequences of the Armenian Genocide*, Cham: Springer.

Hovannisian, R. G. (1986). "The Armenian Genocide and Patterns of Denial." In R. G. Hovannisian (ed.), *The Armenian Genocide in Perspective. Cultural and Ethical Legacies*. New Brunswick, NJ: Transaction Books, 111–133.

Hovannisian, R. G. (1992). *The Armenian Genocide: History, Politics, Ethics*. Cham: Springer.

Hovyan, V. (2011). "Armenian Community in Bulgaria". In *Noravank Foundation*, electronic version. http://www.noravank.am/eng/articles/detail.php?ELEMENT_ID=6105 [8 March 2023].

Ieni, G. (1986). "Le arti figurative e i khatchkar". In: A. Alpago Novello & al. (eds.), *Gli armeni*. Milano: Jaca Book, 260–272.

Iliev, I. (2001). "Čedata na armenskija narod za svobodata na Bǎlgarija". In G. Hayrabedyan (ed.), *Bǎlgari i Armenci zaedno prez vekovete*. Sofia: Tangra, 360–382.

Ivančev, D. P. (1969). *Bǎlgarski periodičen pečat 1844-1944. Anotiran bibliografski ukazatel. Vol 3.* Sofia: Nauka i izkustvo.

Ivančev, I. (2005). *Armencite, sǎdba i migracija (psihologični aspekti)*. Sofia: S.P. Popeto.

Ivanova, N. (2008). *Armenskata kolonija v Plovdiv i nejnata cǎrkva "Surp Kevork"*. Dissertation. Plovdiv: Paisii Hilendarski University.

Jaworski, A. & Thurlow, C. (eds.) (2010). *Semiotic Landscapes: Language, Image, Space*. London & New York: Continuum.

Karanian, M. (2015). *Historic Armenia After 100 Years: Ani, Kars and the Six Provinces of Western Armenia*. Danville: Stone Garden.

Kasabyan, N. & Giligyan, O. (2008). *Bibliografija na armenskite knigi, izdadeni v Bǎlgarija (1885-1944-1989)*. Plovdiv: Narodna Biblioteka "Ivan Vazov".

Kasbarian, S. (2015). "The myth and reality of 'return' – diaspora in the 'homeland'". In *Diaspora* 18 (3), 358–381.

Kevorkyan, A. (2019). *Nasledstvoto ot Tekirdah*. Părvomaj: Komorek.

Kévorkian, R. H. (2006). *The Armenian Genocide: A Complete History*. London-New York: I. B. Tauris.

Kılıçdağı, O. (2010). "The Armenian community of Constantinople in the Late Ottoman Empire". In: R. Hovannisian & S. Payaslian (eds.), *Armenian Constantinople*. Los Angeles, 229–242.

Konstantinova, Y. & Načev, I. (2019). "Armenskata obštnost v socialističeska Bălgarija meždu repatriacijata i amerikanskata mečta". In Y. Konstantinova & I. Načev (eds.), *S pogled kăm Amerika: Izsledvaneto na bălgarski armenci ot socialističeska Bălgarija*. Sofia: Fakel, 25–58.

Koulayan, N. (2006). "Les langues diasporiques et internet: entre nouvelle territorialité, résistance identitaire et partage des savoirs". In *Hermès* 45 (2), 139–145.

Köker, O. (2012). Teotig. *Baskı ve Harf. Ermeni Matbaacılık Tarihi*. Istanbul: Birzamanlar Yayıncılık.

Krasteva, A. (1999). "Ethnicity". In A. Krasteva (ed.), *Communities and Identities in Bulgaria*. Ravenna: Longo editore, 11–40.

Kuciukian, P. (1998). *Dispersi. Viaggio fra le comunità armene del mondo*. Milano: Guerini e Associati.

Kutalmıš, M. (2003). "On Turkish in Armenian Script". In *Journal of Economic and Social Research* 5 (2), 47–59.

Laycock, J. (2012). "The Repatriation of Diaspora Armenians to the Soviet Union, 1945-9". In *Cultural and Social History* IX, 103–123.

Lejean, G. (1867). "Plan der Stadt Filibe". In *Le Tour du Monde* T. 26.

Lepsius, J. (1919). *Der Todesgang des armenischen Volkes: Bericht über das Schicksal des armenischen Volkes in der Türkei während des Weltkrieges*, Potsdam.

Levitt Schiller, G. (2004). "Conceptualizing simultaneity: A transnational social field perspective on society". In *The International Migration Review* 28 (3), 1002–1039.

Linke, U. (2005). "Collective memory, anthropology of". In J.D. Wright (ed.), *The International Encyclopedia of the Social & Behavioral Sciences* 4. Oxford: Elsevier, 181–187.

Maksoudian, F. K. (2006). *The Origins of the Armenian Alphabet and Literature*. New York: St.Vartan Press.

Mandel'štam, O. (1930). *Journey to Armenia*. Selected poems translated into English by Ian Probstein. In *Interliqt* 13. Available at http://interl itq.org/issue13-2/osip-mandelstam/job.php [8 March 2023].

Manoukian, A. (1986). "La struttura sociale del popolo armeno". In: A. Alpago Novello & al. (eds.), *Gli armeni*. Milano: Jaca Book, 69–81.

Markov, G. (2001). "Uvodni dumi". In G. Hayrabedyan (ed.), *Bălgari i Armenci zaedno prez vekovete*. Sofia: Tangra.

Marsden, P. (1994). *The Crossing Place. A Journey among the Armenians*. London: Flamingo.

Maturana, H. & Varela, F. (1984). *El arbol del conocimiento*. Buenos Aires: Lumen.

Mc Luhan, M. (1962). *The Gutenberg Galaxy. The Making of Typographic Man*. Toronto: University of Toronto Press.

Miceva, E. (2001). *Armencite v Bălgarija – Kultura i identičnost*. Sofia: IMIR.

Miceva, E. & Papazian-Tanelian, S. (1998). "Armenians". In A. Krasteva (ed.), *Communities and Identities in Bulgaria*. Ravenna: Longo editore, 111–124.

Miceva, E. & Papazian-Tanielin, S. (2007). *Armencite raskazvat za sebe si....* Sofia: Akademično izdatelstvo Prof. Marin Drinov.

Mikaelian, H. (2010). *Tova koeto iskam da kaža za*. Plovdiv: Matador 74.

Minassian, J. (2020). *Surviving the Forgotten Genocide: An Armenian Memoir*. Lanham: Rowman & Littlefield.

Moore, I. (2019). "Vilnius memoryscape. Razing and raising of monuments, collective memory and national identity". In *Linguistic Landscape* 5 (3), 248–280.

Nora, P. (ed.) (1984). *Les Lieux de mémoire*, Vol. I. Paris: Gallimard.

Ong, W. J. (1982). *Orality and Literacy. The Technologizing of the Word*. London-New York: Routledge.

Ormandjyan, A. (2000). *Armenski Imenik*, Plovdiv: Armen Tur.

Oshagan, V. (1986). "Literature of the Armenian Diaspora". In *World Literature Today* 60 (2): 224–228.

Ozanyan, B. (2003). Mahitaritskoto učilište v Plovdiv văzpitva dostojni graždani na stranata ni. In *Menk. Duhovno i kulturno nasledstvo*. Plovdiv: Erevan & Vahan, 21–23.

Palakian, G. (1922). *Hay Goghgot'an: Druagner Hay martirosagrut'enên, Berlinên dêpi Têr-Zôr, 1914-1920*. Vienna: Mkhit'arean Tparan.

Panossian, R. (1998). "Between ambivalence and intrusion: Politics and identity in Armenia-Diaspora relations". In *Diaspora: A Journal of Transnational Studies* 7 (2), 149–196.

Parekordzagani Tzain. (2004). "Article" (no author). In *Parekordzagani Tzain* 1, 3.

Parekordzagani Tzain. (2006). "Govorete Armenski" (no author). In *Parekordzagani Tzain* 18, 4.

Parekordzagani Tzain. (2015). "Message". In *Parekordzagani Tzain* 147, 1.

Payaslian, S. (2004). "The Armenian resistance at Shabin-Karahisar in 1915". In R.G. Hovannisian (ed.), *Armenian Sebastia. Sivas and Lesser Armenia*. Costa Mesa: Mazda Publishers, 399–426.

Payaslian, S. (2010). "Imagining Armenia". In A. Gal, A.S. Leoussi, & A.D. Smith (eds.), *The Call of the Homeland: Diaspora Nationalisms, Past and Present*. Leiden-Boston: Brill, 105–138.

Papazian-Tanielian, S. (2016). "The community life of Armenians in post-socialist Bulgaria". In K. Siekierski & S. Troebst (eds.), *Armenians in Post-Socialist Europe*. Wien-Cologne: Böhlau Verlag, 193–204.

Peroomian, R. (2003). "New directions in literary responses to the Armenian Genocide". In R.G. Hovannisian (ed.), *Looking Backward, Moving Forward. Confronting the Armenian Genocide*. New Brunswick-London: Routledge, 157–180.

Petrucci, A. (2007). *Prima lezione di Paleografia*. Roma: Laterza.

Rushdie, S. (1991). *Imaginary Homelands. Essays and Criticism 1981-1991*. London: Granta Books.

Safran, W. (1991). "Diasporas in modern societies: Myths of homeland and return". In *Diaspora: A Journal of Transnational Studies* 1, 83–99.

Sahakyan, V. (2018). "Rethinking the Discourse on Armenian Diaspora: Language(s), Culture(s), Affiliation(s)". In *EVN Report*. Available at: https://evnreport.com/raw-unfiltered/rethinking-the-discourse-on-armenian-diaspora-language-s-culture-s-affiliation-s/ [8 March 2023].

Sahakyan, V. (2021). "Diaspora Conceptualizations and the Realities of the Armenian Diaspora: Some Preliminary Observations". In *EVN Report*. Available at: https://evnreport.com/magazine-issues/diaspora-con ceptualizations-and-the-realities-of-the-armenian-diaspora-some-prel iminary-observations/ [8 March 2023].

Salbashyan, O. (2021). *General Karekin. Geroj na dva Naroda*. Plovdiv: Parekordzagan.

Sarkisyan, S. (2007). *Istorija na Armenija*. Sofia: Iztok-Zapad.

Selvelli, G. (2017). "Identity and multiplicity in Canetti's and Wagenstein's birthplaces: Exploring the rhizomatic roots of Europe". In *Bulgarian Studies* 1, 60–85.

Selvelli, G. (2018). "Preserving the postmemory of the Genocide: The Armenian Diaspora's institutions in Plovdiv". In *Acta Universitatis Carolinae – Studia Territorialia* 2, 89–116.

Selvelli, G. (2021). *The Alphabet of Discord. The Ideologization of Writing Systems on the Balkans since the Breakup of Multiethnic Eempires*. Stuttgart: Ibidem.

Selvelli, G. (2023). "The material and symbolic presence of Cyril and Methodius's work in the Bulgarian monumental landscape: affirming and removing the past", In: M. G. Varvounis, N. Macha, & D. Onica (eds.), *Material Culture and Everyday Politics in the Balkans*. Frankfurt: Peter Lang, (in print).

Selvelli, G. (2023b). "Nous écrivons, donc nous existons: identité et mémoire dans le paysages linguistique arménien de Plovdiv". In *Diversité Urbaine* (in print).

Seppälä, S. (2016). "The 'temple of non-being' at Tsitsernakaberd and remembrance of the Armenian Genocide: An interpretation". In *Approaching Religion* 6 (2), 26–39.

Setrakian, S. (2004). "Novo izdanie: Parekordzagani Tzain". In *Parekordzagani Tzain* 1: 2.

Sevan, S. (1996). *Rodosto, Rodosto, Njakăde na Balkanite, Der Zor: Roman-trilogija*. Sofia: Hristo Botev.

Smith, A. D. (1991). *National Identity*. Reno: University of Nevada Press.

Smith, A. D. (1992). "Chosen peoples: Why eyhnic groups survive". In *Ethnic and Racial Studies* 15 (3), 434–456.

Smith, A. D. (1999). "Ethnic election and national destiny: Some religious origins of nationalist ideals". In *Nations and Nationalism* 5 (3), 331–355.

Smith, A. D. (2007). "The power of ethnic traditions in the modern world". In A. S. Leoussi & S. Grosby, Steven (eds.), *Nationalism and Ethnosymbolism. History, Culture and Ethnicity in the Formation of Nations*. Edinburgh: Edinburgh University Press, 325–336.

Smith, A. D. (2009). *Ethno-Symbolism and Nationalism. A Cultural Approach*. London and New York: Routledge.

Stamatov, V. (2001). "Poznavame li se dostatăčno?" In G. Hayrabedyan (ed.), *Bălgari i Armenci zaedno prez vekovete*. Sofia: Tangra.

Strauss, C. L. (1963). *Structural Anthropology*. New York: Basic books [1958].

Tavityan, T. (2021). *Armenians in Bulgaria: Identity and Historical Memory*. Costa Mesa California: Mazda.

Tchilingirian, H. (2018). "What Is 'Armenian' in Armenian Identity?". In *EVN Report*. Available at: https://evnreport.com/raw-unfiltered/what-is-armenian-in-armenian-identity/ [8 March 2023].

Todorov, T. (1977). *Theories du Symbole*. Paris: Editions Seuil.

Topakbashyan, V. (2003). "1600 godini ni delyat ot sătvorjavaneto im. Armenskite pismena". In *Menk. Religija – Cărkovna obrednost*. Plovdiv: Vahan & Erevan, 31–33, 41.

Tölölyan, K. (1996). 'Rethinking diaspora(s): Stateless power in the transnational moment'. In *Diaspora: A Journal of Transnational Studies* 5(2), 3–36.

Tölölyan, K. (2000). "Elites and Institutions in the Armenian Transnation". In *Diaspora: A Journal of Transnational Studies* 9 (1), 107–136

Tölölyan, K. (2002). *Redefining Diasporas: Old Approaches, New Identities*. London: Armenian Institute.

Tölölyan, K. & Papazian, T. (2014). "Armenian diasporas and Armenia: Issues of identity and mobilization". In *Études armeniennes contemporaines* 3, 83–101.

Tumanyan, H. (1997). *David Sasunski. Poema*. Plovdiv: Armen Tur.

Turan, Z. & Bakalian, A. (2015). "Diaspora tourism and identity: Subversion and consolation in Armenian pilgrimages to eastern Turkey".

In A. Gorman & S. Kasbarian (eds.), *Diasporas of the Modern Middle East: Contextualising Community*. Edinburgh: Edinburgh University Press, 173–211.

Turner, J. C., Brown, R. J., & Tajfel, H. (1979). "Social comparison and group interest in ingroup favouritism". In *European Journal of Social Psychology* 9 (2), 187–204.

Tutunjyan. (1994). *Booklet published on occasion of the 160th anniversary since the founding of the Viktoria and Krikor Tutunjyan School*. Plovdiv.

Uluhogian, G. (1999). "Lingua e cultura scritta". In A.A.V.V. *Gli Armeni*. Milano: Jaca Book, 115–130.

Vahan. (2010). "Article on the Armenian alphabet" (no author). In *Vahan*, 19 October 2010 (in Armenian).

Van Hear, N. (1998). *New Diasporas. The Mass Exodus, Dispersal and Regrouping of Migrant Communities*. London: UCL Press.

Vardanyan, V. (2021). *National Identity, Diaspora and Space of Belonging. An Armenian Perspective*. London: Gomidas Institute.

Vetsigian, S. (1943). *Šapin K'arahisari badmowt'yownə*. Unpublished manuscript: Plovdiv.

Vetsigian, S. (2001). *Voden ot Boga v služba na naroda si*, Plovdiv. Plovdiv: Armen Tur.

Vetsigian, S. (2014). *Autobiography. His Guiding Hand to Serve My People*. Plovdiv: Parekordzagan.

Viviano, F. (2004). "Našite vojnici". In *Parekordzagani Tzain* 1, 3.

Voillery, P. (2012). *Alexandre Exarh. Un destin bulgare*. Istanbul: ISIS Press.

Wagenstein, A. (2002). *Daleč ot Toledo*. Sofia: Colibri.

Walker, C. J. (2005). *Visions of Ararat, Writings on Armenia*. New York: Tauris.

Zarecka, I. I. (1994). *Frames of Remembrance: The Dynamics of Collective Memory*. New Jersey: Transaction Publishers.

Zarzavatdjian, R. & Zarzavatdjian, C. (2017). *Cuisine d'Armenie*. Paris: Solar.

Zekiyan, B. L. (1997). *The Armenian Way to Modernity. Armenian Identity Between Tradition and Innovation, Specificity and Universality*. Venezia: Supernova.

Zekiyan, B. L. (1997b). "L'identitè polyvalente dans le tèmoignage d'un artiste: Sergueï Paradjanov. Reflexions sur le problème de la polyvalence ethnique et culturelle". In *Acta Orientalia 50* (1–3), 337–347.

Zekiyan, B. L. (2000). *L'Armenia e gli armeni. Polis lacerata e patria spirituale: la sfida di una sopravvivenza*. Milano: Guerini e associati.

Zekiyan, B.L. (2013). "Venezia, il luogo delle 'rivelazioni' della Provvidenza per gli Armeni. Riflessioni a partire dal modello armeno per un possibile nuovo concetto d'identità dalle dialettiche antagonistiche verso una integrazione differenziata". In G. Pedrini (ed.), *Studia Orientis. Venezia e l'Oriente. Un'eredità culturale*. Vicenza: Editrice Veneta, 75–102.

Zerubavel, E. (2004). *Time Maps: Collective Memory and the Social Shape of the Past*. Chicago: University of Chicago Press.

Zlatkova, M. (2023). "Tjutjun, metal i kăldăram: setivost, pamet i nematerialno nasledstvo v grada". In B. Petkova & V. Karadžov (eds.), *Kapanite na grada*. Plovdiv: Plovdivsko Universitetsko Izdatelstvo, 12–32.

Illustrations

Band 22 BESTERS-DILGER, Juliane (Hg.): Kommentierter Apostolos. Textedition und Kommentar zur Edition. (= Die großen Lesemenäen des Metropoliten Makarij Uspenskij Spisok.) Unter Mitarbeit von V. Halapats, N. Kindermann, E. Maier, A. Rabus. 2014.

Band 23 ILIĆ, Marija: Discourse and Ethnic Identity. The Case of the Serbs from Hungary. 2014.

Band 24 HLAVAC, Jim; FRIEDMANN, Victor (Hrsg.): On Macedonian Matters: from the Partition and Annexation of Macedonia in 1913 to the Present. A Collection of Essays on Language, Culture and History. 2015.

Band 25 HLAVAC, Jim: Three generations, two countries of origin, one speech community: Australian-Macedonians and their language(s). 2016.

Band 26 GÖRBES, Tamás; HEGEDÜS, Rita: Small Language, what now?. The Theory and Practice of Functional Linguistics in Teaching "Minor" Languages.

Band 27 TYRAN, Katharina Klara: Identitäre Verortungen entlang der Grenze. Verhandlungen von Sprache und Zugehörigkeit bei den Burgenländischen Kroaten. 2015.

Band 28 LORMES, Miriam: „Among good musicians there has never been an ethnical divide". Interkulturalität und politisches Engagement in Musikerdiskursen im postjugoslawischen Makedonien. 2013.

Band 29 GLANC, Tomáš und VOSS, Christian (Hrsg.): Konzepte des Slawischen. 2016.

Band 30 GEHRKE, Stefan: Jedwabne und die Folgen. Eine semantische Analyse der Debatte über Juden in der polnischen Presse 2001–2008. 2018.

Band 31 STERN, Dieter; NOMACHI, Motoki; BELIĆ, Bojan (eds.): Linguistic regionalism in eastern europe and beyond. Minority, Regional and Literary Microlanguages. In memoriam Jiří Marvan. 2018.

Band 32 RAJILIĆ, Simone: Weiblichkeit im Serbischen. Weibliche Genderspezifizierungen zwischen Gewalt und Widerstand. 2019.

Band 33 SCHELLER-BOLTZ, Dennis: Grammatik und Ideologie. Feminisierungsstrategien im Russischen und Polnischen aus Sicht der Wissenschaft und Gesellschaft. 2020.

Band 34 FRIEDMAN, Victor; JANEV, Goran; VLAHOV, George (eds.): Macedonia & Its Questions. Origins, Margins, Ruptures & Continuity. 2020.

Band 35 MUJADŽEVIĆ, Dino (ed.): Digital Historical Research on Southeast Europe and the Ottoman Space. 2021.

Band 36 DANOVA, Tsvetomira: John of Damascus' Marian Homilies in Mediaeval South Slavic Literatures. 2020.

Band 37 JOURAVEL, Anna; MATHYS, Audrey (eds.): Wort- und Formenvielfalt. Festschrift für Christoph Koch zum 80. Geburtstag. Unter Mitarbeit von Daniel Petit. 2021.

Band 38 ČAPO, Jasna: Zwei Zuhause. Kroatische Arbeitsmigration nach Deutschland als transnationales Phänomen. 2022.

Band 39 FOTIADIS, Ruza; VOSS, Christian: Sprachliche Grenzziehungen in der griechisch-mazedonischen Kontaktzone im 20. Jahrhundert. 2023.

Band 40 VOSS, Christian; JUSUFI, Lumnije; REUTER, Evelyn (eds.): Innovative Paths of Albanology. Proceedings of the Early Career Researcher Conference on 14th and 15th October 2021. 2023.

Band 41 KÜHNEL, Ferdinand; MICOLOVÁ, Soňa; STANKOVIĆ, Snežana: (eds.): East Central European Cemeteries. Ethnic, Linguistic, and Narrative Aspects of Sepulchral Culture and the Commemoration of the Dead in Borderlands. 2023.

Band 42   BURLACU, Constanta: Biblical Books in the Romanian Lands in the Sixteenth Century. A Textual Analysis of Apostolos and Psalter Texts. Forthcoming.

Band 43   ČEMERNICA, Aldina: Bosnien als Herkunftsland – Berlin als „Heimat": Identitätskonstruktionen junger Menschen bosnischer/bosniakischer Herkunft in Berlin. 2023.

Band 44   SELVELLI, Giustina: Language Attitudes, Collective Memory and (Trans)National Identity Construction Among the Armenian Diaspora in Bulgaria. 2024.

www.peterlang.com

Milton Keynes UK
Ingram Content Group UK Ltd.
UKHW021909080324
438955UK00008B/28